Relational Discipleship

Cross Training

Books by Paul J. Bucknell

Allowing the Bible to speak to our lives today!

+ Overcoming Anxiety: Finding Peace, Discovering God
+ Reaching Beyond Mediocrity: Being an Overcomer
+ The Life Core: Discovering the Heart of Great Training
+ The Godly Man: When God Touches a Man's Life
+ Redemption Through the Scriptures
+ Godly Beginnings for the Family
+ Principles and Practices of Biblical Parenting
+ Building a Great Marriage
+ Christian Premarital Counseling Manual for Counselors
+ Relational Discipleship: Cross Training
+ Running the Race: Overcoming Lusts
+ Genesis: The Book of Foundations
+ Book of Romans: The Living Commentary
+ Book of Romans: Bible Study Questions
+ Bible Study Questions for the Book of Ephesians
+ Walking with Jesus: Abiding in Christ
+ Inductive Bible Studies in Titus
+ 1 Peter Bible Study Questions: Living in a Fallen World
+ Take Your Next Step into Ministry
+ Training Leaders for Ministry
+ Study Guide for Jonah: Understanding God's Heart

Check out these valuable resources at
www.foundationsforfreedom.net

RELATIONAL DISCIPLESHIP

Cross Training

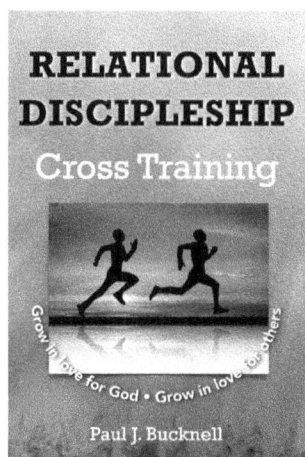

RELATIONAL
DISCIPLESHIP
Cross Training

Grow in love for God • Grow in love for others

Paul J. Bucknell

Paul J. Bucknell

Relational Discipleship: Cross Training

Copyright © July, 2010, 2014 Paul J. Bucknell
Pittsburgh, PA 15212 USA

ISBN-10: 1619930307
ISBN-13: 978-1-61993-030-8

E-Book:
ISBN-10: 1619930315
ISBN-13: 978-1-61993-031-5

The NASB version is used unless otherwise stated.
New American Standard Bible ©1960, 1995 used by permission,
Lockman Foundation www.lockman.org.

Paul Bucknell has written extensively on many of these topics and further resources such as powerpoints, check out our Discipleship (D1) Training Library at www.foundationsforfreedom.net .

www.foundationsforfreedom.net

Appreciation

*We give praise to God
who strengthens our hands,
washes our sin,
provides wisdom, and
governs our circumstances
so to make us strong and
reflect His glory!*

Table of Contents

Preface

God's people urgently need to be discipled! This is getting to be more true as societies around the world are increasingly plagued with dysfunctional families. Believers have a hard time understanding what is proper or even possible in various relationships.

The real problem is rooted in a spirit of apathy in the church in its responsibility to disciple her people. Those who disciple fellow believers are an exception. The situation is the same worldwide. There is, then, both a lack of vision for discipleship which has created this great need for personal basic training. The Book of Titus attests to this problem by pointing to the solution (Titus 2:1-10) – Raise up men and women of character who will train the young believers. Discipleship is an imperative (Matthew 28:18-20)!

Through this twelve-part biblical series you should be able to make disciples, and especially equip those who have grown up in difficult family situations. By learning and applying the basic truths that lay behind having good relationships with God and man, God's people will live righteous and enriched Christian lives.

I myself grew up in a dysfunctional home. Divorce along with bitterness was accepted as the norm. I had to struggle through so many personal problems. How I wish I had someone to disciple me. Instead I had to wrestle with these personal problems myself, greatly multiplying my failures.

Just like a baby, a new believer needs to be personally nurtured by God's Word. The *Relational Discipleship* course leads God's people into how to properly relate to others which they might otherwise never see. This book is designed to provide the believer a biblically sound perspective on how proper relationships function and thus provides a strong foundation for the believer's spiritual life.

Each chapter provides a new opportunity for disciple-makers to discuss possible problems that the disciple might be facing in that area of life. Jesus purposely used familiar illustrations to lead His people on a deeper walk. The father-child, husband-wife, vine-branches, judge-sinners, shepherd-lamb are a few examples. Christ is our supreme example to lead us further along.

Now is the time that we begin to train all believers to grow in love for God and for others. Take your part in this great work of God. Be a disciple-maker. *Relational Discipleship* and other associated resources provide life illustrations, biblically sound teaching, helpful diagrams, deep and enriching insights to help the new believer develop that deeply needed strong spiritual foundation. The appendices supplies other helpful tools on using the resources and its objective.

July 2010, updated 2014
Paul J. Bucknell
Pittsburgh, Pennsylvania, USA

#1 Father ⬌ Child

Growing in love
for God and others!

FATHER

CHILD

Resembling our father

Father and Child

Resembling Our Father

Jesus the Son fully trusted His Father to care for all His personal and ministry needs. In the same way we are to imitate Jesus by trusting and obeying our Heavenly Father. Our lives will then greatly reflect our Father's love through our care to those around us.

The Model Son

Our ideas of God greatly influence our trust in Him. Some people think of God as cold and distant. They are reluctant to trust Him. Others believe He is harsh and waiting to find fault. They find it difficult to develop a close relationship with Him, but how did Jesus think of His Father?

Jesus had such a special relationship with the Father and wants us to have one too. In His model prayer Jesus instructs us to address the Almighty God as "Our Father." God is a perfect Father who provides love, care, guidance and correction for His children. As we learn these truths, we can better trust Him.

So just as Jesus models the perfect son by trusting, obeying and resembling His Father, so we can live like Jesus and share a close relationship with God and other believers too. *"Holy Father, keep them in Thy name, the name which Thou has given Me, that they may be one, even as We are" (John 17:11).*

Our Goals

A	God is Jesus' Father	➡	Learn how God is our Father
B	Jesus is His firstborn Son	➡	Trust and obey like Jesus did
C	We are children of God	➡	Let others see the Father through us

A God is Our Father

God is Jesus' Father

1) The Father loves the Son.

God described Jesus at the beginning of His ministry, "*This is My beloved Son, in whom I am well-pleased*" (Matthew 3:17). Circle below the words in the quote that the Father uses to describe Jesus.

For the Father Himself loves you, because you have loved Me and have believed that I came forth from the Father. (John 16:27)

Like Jesus, we too have the immense privilege of being called the sons of God and sharing in the Father's love. Jesus Himself said to His disciples. God *loves* you! He doesn't see you as a sinner anymore, but as one of His *sons*!

2) The Father takes care of the Son.

Once one of Christ's disciples tried to protect Jesus. Jesus exclaimed, "*Don't you realize that I could ask my Father for thousands of angels to protect us, and he would send them instantly?*"(Matthew 26:52-53 NLT)

God the Father always watches over the needs of His children. As Creator He is more powerful than any enemy we might face.

Read Matthew 6:7-8 below. What did Jesus teach about how the Father cares for them?

And when you are praying, do not use meaningless repetition, as the Gentiles do, for they suppose that they will be heard for their many words. Therefore do not be like them; for your Father knows what you need, before you ask Him.

From the verses above, what does Jesus say about talking to your Father?

1. Don't use _____.

2. Our Father knows _____.

We need to learn to immediately take every problem or need to our Father instead of worrying about it. As a little child I never worried about my food or clothes. My father made sure I had what I needed. He cared for me.

3) The Father directs and trains the Son.

Jesus spent much time talking to His Father in prayer. Jesus liked spending time with His Heavenly Father and doing what He wanted. Once He said this, *"For I have come down from heaven, not to do My own will, but the will of Him who sent Me"* (John 6:38).

Our Father wants to make us like Him. He shows us His will through the Bible, parents and teachers that love Him. Sometimes the training also comes through difficult circumstances! We need to be attentive and obedient.

Application
Tell your heavenly Father about your day today. Identify a need you have and trustingly ask Him to take care of it.

B   **Responding to our Father**

Jesus is His Firstborn Son

We gain precious insight into a son's proper mindset from Jesus' own example. Jesus Christ took His role as a son very seriously.

1) The Son honors His Father.

Over and over when Jesus healed somebody that person gave God the glory. Once Jesus prayed, *"Father, glorify Your name." (John 12:28)*

Jesus always sought to bring attention, honor and glory to His Father. Notice what Jesus said in the Sermon on the Mount,

> *Let your light shine before men in such a way that they may see your good works, and glorify your Father who is in heaven. (Matthew 5:16)*

● Circle the word 'glorify' above.

● Finish the sentence "Glorify _____ who is in heaven."

Who are we taught to honor? Us? No! Our Father in heaven! We deliberately need to bring Him the glory because He is the One doing great things.

2) The Son trusts and obeys His Father.

God gives us a great promise, *"And we know that God causes all things to work together for good to those who love God..."* (Romans 8:28).

Those things may not always be pleasant or easy, but nothing is ever out of God's control. He can even use painful and confusing situations to cause a greater good for us and others than otherwise could happen.

A brother's testimony:

"Once, I was looking for a job and found an interesting but low paying one. That particular job wouldn't have met my financial needs for the upcoming school year. My father asked me to turn it down, promising he would lend me money while I continued to search. I could have held on to the sure job that I had but decided to trust my heavenly Father to provide me with a better job as I obeyed Him by obeying my earthly father. God gave me a special peace about giving up that one sure job and ultimately provided me with the best internship I've ever had!"

3) The Son depends on His Father.

Jesus was very dependent upon His Father's provision. So are we, but we can always trust God to care for us. Jesus says, *"If you then, being evil, know how to give good gifts to your children, how much more will your Father who is in heaven give what is good to those who ask Him"* (Matthew 7:11)!

Our Father wants to bless us (although not always how we expect). He cares for our well-being. We need to learn to often ask for His blessing! Our Father loves to work in response to our prayers.

Application

Identify an area of your life that hasn't been honoring to your Father. Seek to change your attitudes and ways. Pray for His help.

C Resembling Our Father

We are sons of God

You might have heard the saying, *"Like father, like son."* You can tell things about someone's dad by the way his son acts. Jesus was a perfect demonstration of His Father's character. One of Jesus' disciples once asked Him to show him the Father. Jesus' reply was,

Have I been so long with you, and yet you have not come to know Me, Philip? He who has seen Me has seen the Father; how can you say, 'Show us the Father'? (John 14:8-9)

As we come to know our Father more deeply, we will want to be more like Him. The family resemblance should be so strong that others see the Father in us. Here are some ways others should see our Heavenly Father in our lives:

1) Doing His Works

We read earlier in Matthew 5:16 that we should do good _____ so the Father gets the glory. We look for opportunities to cheerfully serve others.

2) Making Peace

Jesus in Matthew 5:9 said, *"Blessed are the peacemakers, for they shall be called _____."* We must not only refuse to angrily argue with others but graciously introduce God's peace and love into our relationships.

3) Loving enemies

Look up Matthew 5:44-45 and fill in the missing words, *"But I say to you, love your enemies and pray for those who persecute you, so that you may be _____ who is in heaven; for He causes His sun to rise on the evil and the good, and sends rain on the righteous and the unrighteous."*

As God's children, we are to be just as merciful as our Heavenly Father. It's hard! We need His love. God will give us this love as we seek Him for it.

4) Loving one another

Our relationship with our Father should directly translate into love and care for others in God's family. No sibling rivalry allowed! "Beloved, let us love one another, for love is from God; and everyone who loves is born of God and knows God. The one who does not love does not know God, for God is love" (1 John 4:7-8).

5) **Expanding God's family**

God wants a big family! Jesus fulfilled what His Father purposed for Him. But there is still more work! He now sends us out to finish the work. "*As You sent Me into the world, so I also have sent them into the world" (John 17:18).*

Application

(1) Bring to mind a person you have been an enemy with. Ask your Father to give you His amazing love for this individual. Then do something pleasant for that person.

(2) Who is the Lord urging you to share the Gospel with so that the Father might work through your life to bring someone to know Him just as He did with Jesus?

Summary

A) Our Father loves, provides for and guides us.

B) Knowing and loving our Father makes trust and obedience desirable and natural.

C) As we become more like our Father, others will notice the resemblance through our love for others.

Take Home Projects

• **Memory Verses**   **1 John 3:1**

See how great a love the Father has bestowed upon us, that we should be called children of God; and such we are. (NASB)

• **Prayer Journal**

Take time to write down your worries, concerns and needs in your spiritual journal. Write down the date and time. Specifically ask God to satisfy those needs. When He answers, write down the way He answered those prayers along with the date and time.

· Make peace with your earthly father

We are to honor our father and mother. If you have unconfessed sin towards your father, first pray and ask your parents for forgiveness. Make sure you ask for an apology, "Will you please forgive me?"

· Interview

Ask a mature believer to share about one or two incidents in their lives where God specially cared for him as his Father. Note what the struggle was and how God supplied His provision, wisdom, or encouragement to him.

· Loving Others

Find another believer and demonstrate God's love by encouraging or doing something special for that person.

#2 Shepherd ⟷ Lamb

*Growing in love
for God and others!*

Shepherd and Lamb

Reflecting God's love in our lives

The Shepherd–Lamb image powerfully communicates God's good care for His people. He is our Shepherd who genuinely cares for us. He sent Christ to die for us. It was the only way He could make us His own, and since we are His, He lavishes His love upon us. This powerful sense of caring so transforms our lives that we are expected to extend His care to others.

Finding Our Way Home

We all long for those deep intimate friendships. Have you ever thought about being close to God? God has. He cares for you! Notice how He speaks about His relationship with His disciples.

No longer do I call you slaves, for the slave does not know what his master is doing; but I have called you friends, for all things that I have heard from My Father I have made known to you (John 15:15).

Christ set a wonderful example of a good shepherd. He did everything that was needed to bring the sheep (us–God's people) into the fold, to protect and provide for them.

For this is what the sovereign Lord says: "*I myself will search for my sheep and look for them.*" I will rescue "*them from all the places where they were scattered on a day of clouds and darkness*" (Ezekiel 34:11,12).

Jesus Christ as the 'Lamb of God' demonstrated a wonderful model for us. As a sheep He listened and fully trusted His Shepherd. He willingly bore the cross and died a painful death for our sins. As the Lamb of God he teaches us the proper attitude towards obedience of God's commands. Most remarkably He showed us how to allow Him to perform His good will in and through our lives. The Good Shepherd leads us in God's good ways. We only need to follow. Why wouldn't we?

> *I am the good shepherd; and I know My own, and My own know Me, even as the Father knows Me and I know the Father; and I lay down My life for the sheep (John 10:14-15).*

Our Goals

A	God provides a good Shepherd ⟹	Rejoice in God's goodness
B	Christ is our Shepherd; we are His sheep ⟹	Trust God completely
C	We are to extend God's love to others ⟹	Love others unconditionally

---

A God Provides a Shepherd
Rejoice in a Good Shepherd

There might be many things that we do not understand in this world but behind it all we must have a strong belief that God is good. God really cares about wayward man. We see this in a number of ways.

1) We strayed from God

We are all like sheep that strayed from the shepherd and were vulnerable to attack. *"And they were scattered for lack of a shepherd, and they became food for every beast of the field and were scattered" (Ezekiel 34:5).* This speaks about Adam's original sin, but also reveals how all of us choose to live out a life different apart from

God's good commands. Do you sense that bent to do wrong in your own life? This is called the sinful nature.

2) There was none to help

It is bad enough being helpless, but no one could help. "My flock wandered through all the mountains and on every high hill, and My flock was scattered over all the surface of the earth; and there was no one to search or seek for them" (Ezekiel 34:6). No one really cared. Isn't that the way many people feel today? Everyone is out for himself.

3) Religious leaders didn't help

Even religious leaders can disappoint us. God had appointed leaders over His people to care for them, but even these leaders in many cases sought their own good. They were lazy and indulgent. "My flock has even become food for all the beasts of the field for lack of a shepherd, and My shepherds did not search for My flock, but rather the shepherds fed themselves and did not feed My flock" (Ezekiel 34:8).

Some people turn their hearts away from God because their religious leader failed them. Do you think this is right? What should the right response be? Did a leader ever disappoint you?

4) God Himself Would care for His people

How strange and wonderful that God reached out to care for the very ones that offended and defied Him. *"For thus says the Lord GOD, 'Behold, I Myself will search for My sheep and seek them out'"* (Ezekiel 34:11).

God cares for His people by making sure that they have the best pasture land. "I will feed them in a good pasture, and their grazing ground will be on the mountain heights of Israel" (Ezekiel 34:14). How did He do this? He Himself would appoint a faithful shepherd.

This Good Shepherd would be His own Son that He would send from heaven to live among men and die for His people. "Then I will set over them one shepherd, My servant David, and he will feed them; he will feed them himself and be their shepherd" (Ezekiel 34:23). Jesus Christ came in David's lineage.

Application

How grateful we should be to our God for searching us out! We might search for our favorite things, but would we go out of our way to look for that which was broken and dirty? Thank the Lord for having Jesus die on the cross so we could be added us to His flock.

B Christ is Our Shepherd

Trust Christ as sheep trust their shepherd

Sheep are not know for being clever. Their lives are dependent upon how well the shepherd cares for them and to what degree they follow the shepherd. Jesus is our wonderful shepherd that cares for us.

1) A Shepherd Knows

A good shepherd knows His sheep. Jesus said, *"I am the good shepherd; and I know My own, and My own know Me"* (John 10:14). Acquiring knowledge of a person is the first step of knowing a person's real needs. Jesus knows His sheep.

2) A Shepherd Provides

The Lord is my Shepherd, I shall not want. He makes me lie down in green pastures; He leads me beside still waters (Psalm 23:1-2).

In the verse above circle who is our shepherd. Underline two things the shepherd makes the sheep do?

Sheep fully rely on their shepherd for what they need. A good shepherd prepares the pasture for his sheep by making sure there are no harmful things in it. A lamb will not lie down unless it is fully satisfied and feeling secure.

Jesus calls himself the Good Shepherd (John 10:11). As your Shepherd, He promises that you will not suffer need. He will provide for everything (Matthew 6:25-26). He does not promise to meet all our desires, though. If we completely trust Jesus to provide, then we won't worry about our seemingly difficult circumstances.

3) A Shepherd Protects

Even though I walk through the Valley of the Shadow of Death, I will fear no evil; for Thou art with me; The rod and staff they comfort me (Psalm 23:4).

Name some fears you have. Fill in the blanks below with your answers.

"Even though _____, I will fear no evil for Thou art with me."

"Even though _____, I will fear no evil for Thou art with me."

"Even though _____, I will fear no evil for Thou art with me."

Jesus is always there to protect His sheep. Just like a good shepherd will fight wolves and other predators to protect them, so He will watch over us. When we worry about life, a job, our health, or other needs, we show that we are putting our trust in our circumstances rather than God.

The Lord is my Shepherd

Application

We need to pay closer attention to how God provides for us. Share two or three ways the Lord took special care of you in the last week. Say a prayer and thank Him for taking care of you as His lamb.

C

Extend God's Love
Unconditionally love others

Just as Christ our shepherd laid down His life for us, we ought to do whatever is necessary to care for the needs of those God brings into our lives. This is true for a relative, friend, brother, colleague, stranger or neighbor.

1) God's Command For Us to Love Others

Loving others is a command from God. As children of God, we are enabled to love others because God's love fills our hearts.

God has poured out His love into our hearts by the Holy Spirit, whom he has given us (Romans 5:5).

Dear friends, let us love one another, for love comes from God (1 John 4:7).

Notice how God commands us to love others as we love ourselves. *"For the whole Law is fulfilled in one word, in the statement, "'You shall love your neighbor as yourself"* (Galatians 5:14).

Love is the opposite to self-centered living. We need to retrain ourselves to consider the needs of others above ourselves and to be attentive to those needs.

2) Seeking Other Sheep

Jesus said, *"I have other sheep, which are not of this fold; I must bring them also"* (John 10:16). Jesus was speaking mostly of non-Jews here.

How does Jesus bring those sheep into the fold? Give one or two examples of someone doing this.

3) The Need to Love Others in Truth and in Action

If anyone has material possession and sees his brother in need but has no pity on him, how can the love of God be in him? Dear children, let us not love with words or tongue but with actions and in truth. (1 John 3 17-18)

It is very easy for us to say to someone that we love and care for them, but how often do we really pour out our love for them in action? Jesus demonstrated His love for us in action by dying on the cross to save us from eternal death. How can we love others in action today? We can spend time with them, pray for or with them, and give them a helping hand when they are in need.

As God's children, we must love others in action and in truth, so that God can be glorified through our testimony.

Application

1) Identify any 'sheep' that you are responsible to show God's love to. This might include children, a widow, spouse or some friend.

2) Do you think of your responsibility to provide spiritual care to others? A pastor of course must 'pastor' God's people, but God has also given all of His disciples the responsibility to be part of the means He shows spiritual care to others (Matthew 28:18). Name one or two ways that you spiritually care for others.

Summary

A) Get to know and serve God better.

B) Trust more in God's care for you.

C) Love others as God loves you.

Take Home Projects

• **Memory Verse: John 10:14-15**

I am the good shepherd; and I know My own, and My own know Me, even as the Father knows Me and I know the Father; and I lay down My life for the sheep.

- **Develop a God-attentiveness**

Learn to developer a deeper trust in God by observing how He takes care of you. One person recently shared with me how the other day his wife felt overwhelmed with the things going on. He took this need to God in prayer. The Lord cancelled an evening meeting which enabled him to stay home and help his wife. God does many special things like this. Unfortunately, we do not pray and consequently do not see how God works out such situations.

Write out needs that you know of in a journal and pray (make sure you include the need of others). Observe how God cares for each matter. Write the answer to prayer next to the request along with the date. Be attentive: some answers come in unexpected ways and times.

Date Need	Date Answer
✳	
✳	

· **Pass on the Shepherd's love**

Call at least one friend and one relative this week. See how they have been lately and start praying for or with them. Also plan to spend time with them and help them when they need help.

✳ **Friend:**   ✳ **Relative:**

#3 Teacher ◄► Disciple

*Growing in love
for God and others!*

Teacher and Disciple

Learning like Christ

Jesus amazes us not only with His teaching but also with the determined way He set His heart to learn from the Father. If we can see the connection between the two, then we also can set ourselves on a path of transformation. We can brush the dust of the world from our hearts through the golden truths of heaven. How precious it is to think that we can take these lofty truths and pass them on to others!

Learning the Right Way

Many people pay much money and make huge sacrifices to attend the best schools so that they can acquire the best education possible, but in fact, there is no better teacher than God. *"Behold, God is exalted in His power; who is a teacher like Him?"* (*Job 36:22*)

After all, our Lord fully understands the scope and solution to mankind's problems. He is the source of all wisdom. He not only has knowledge of the physical world but also the spiritual world. He understands how everything is interconnected because He made and maintains them. In the end God reveals all truth.

Jesus sets the model for us on how to learn. This is what made Him the greatest teacher. *"And they were amazed at His teaching; for He was teaching them as one having authority, and not as the scribe"* (Mark 1:22). **A great teacher must first be a great learner.** A great learner must be willing to allow the truth of God to shape His life.

Who is a teacher like Him?

32

God desires that we learn His truth. This is the reason He has revealed His principles both in nature as well as in His Word. To the degree that we apply His teaching to our lives, we will be aided by His wisdom and guarded from evil and its consequences. As we are shaped by His Word, we become more like Jesus who allowed the truth of God to shape His life and passed on the Word of Life to others both by word and example.

Our Goals

A — Christ learned from the Father ⟹ **Listen like Jesus**

B — Christians are Christ's disciples ⟹ **Follow Christ alone**

C — Christians make other disciples ⟹ **Make disciples like Jesus**

A | Listening like Christ

Christ continued to meet with the Father

The best teacher is the best learner. This was certainly true in Jesus' life. Because Jesus humbled Himself when He took human form, His Godhead powers were hidden while He was on earth. Therefore, He is an excellent model for us to learn from. Notice His learning spirit in the following verse.

The Lord GOD has given Me the tongue of disciples, that I may know how to sustain the weary one with a word. He awakens Me morning by morning, He awakens My ear to listen as a disciple. (Isaiah 50:4)

1) The tongue of disciple

The modern word for 'disciple' is learner. Jesus became a great teacher by applying Himself to learning. Jesus was a master at asking the right questions. Twelve-year-old Jesus confounded the teachers of the Law with His wisdom.

2) The purpose of the disciple

Jesus' purpose was to learn to help the needy. Many people learn for the wrong reasons: reputation, money, status or fun. Christ's reason for learning was to serve others. He learned well so that He could serve others well.

3) The discipline of the disciple

The faithful disciple doesn't make excuses. Each day He spends time with the Lord. Each morning He eagerly seeks what God His Father would teach Him. There is no vacation from learning from the Lord.

4) The ear of a disciple

Jesus anticipated how God's Words would help Him day by day. He learned everything He needed from the Father. An ear that has been trained through repetitive learning can readily discern what is being communicated.

Each disciple of Christ must start here with a goal of being like His Master. There is no question that our Master wants us to know the Truth, but do we have a passionate desire to be thoroughly influenced and changed by the Truth?

Jesus' parents found Him in the temple, sitting in the midst of the teachers, both listening to them, and asking them questions. And all who heard Him were amazed at His understanding and His answers. (Luke 2:46-47)

Jesus wanted to know the truth. He desired to learn it so that He could carry out His Father's work of satisfying the needs of others. He arranged His activities so that He could hear from His Father. He expected to hear all that He needed to know.

Application

- Learn from your Father. Train yourself to listen to Him. Commit yourself to meeting with Him every morning. In a protected quiet time, anticipate that He will provide for your needs throughout the day.

- Anticipate His Provisions! Make that commitment in a **prayer**. "Dear Father, thank you so much for caring for me. I so desperately need You to teach me. I yearn for you to meet with me early each day to equip me to care for those you bring into my life just like You did with Jesus. In Christ's name I pray, Amen."

B | Walking after Christ

Christians are Christ's disciples

1) The Meaning of Disciple

A disciple literally means 'a learner.' As Christians we learn from Jesus Christ. Those we have learned from leave the greatest affect upon our lives. Note the three kinds of disciples in the following verse. Underline them.

> *And John's disciples and the Pharisees were fasting; and they came and said to Him, "Why do John's disciples and the disciples of the Pharisees fast, but Your disciples do not fast?" (Mark 2:18)*

A Christian by definition should only learn from Christ. The Lord has appointed pastors and teachers to help us learn more. But be careful, not everyone who claims to be a pastor or Christian teacher genuinely loves the Lord.

Soon after Christ left the earth, the word disciple faded from common usage. The word 'Christian' and other terms like 'brother' took its place. Acts 11:26 says, *"The disciples were first called Christians in Antioch."* The term 'Christian' means a follower or adherent of Christ Jesus, literally 'little Christ.'

2) The Success of Christ's Disciple

Jesus said, *"I am the Way, the Truth and the Life" (John 14:6)*. The growth of your Christian life depends upon how much you cleanse yourself of old thoughts which run counter to Christ's teaching and adopt what He says. Do we have to listen to everything that Jesus says? If He really is from God (and He is), it would be foolish to do anything other than what He commands. Notice in the following verses how Jesus demands our full allegiance.

> *As a result of this many of His disciples withdrew, and were not walking with Him anymore. Jesus said therefore to the twelve, "You do not want to go away also, do you?" Simon Peter answered Him, "Lord, to whom shall we go? You have words of eternal life. And we have believed and have come to know that You are the Holy One of God." (John 6:66-69)*

Application

Confirm your allegiance to Jesus Christ your Teacher by both rejecting other teachings and influential teachers and affirming your loyalty to Christ. Mention at least one of your old admired teachers, teachings, religions, philosophies, books, songs, stars, historic or present important figures.

Write down two 'old' things that affected your life. Cross them out as a symbolic gesture that you will no longer allow:

(1) _____

(2) _____

> *I choose Christ Jesus and His principles of love and righteousness above all else.*

Sign & date _____

C   **Making Disciples of Christ**

Christians are living stones

Christ's disciples made other disciples of Christ

1) Christ's Choice of Us

Christ chose the twelve disciples who later became apostles. Later He sent out seventy disciples. Most relevant to us, however, is the charge He gave all of His disciples in each Gospel: proclaim His Gospel (Good News) to others. Discipleship is the process God's people learn more of Christ's teaching and become conformed to His likeness. Read Christ's goal for us.

> *A pupil (disciple) is not above his **teacher**; but everyone, after he has been fully trained, will be like his **teacher**. (Luke 6:40)*

2) Christ's Goals for Us

Christ's goals for us is clear. We will not be greater than our teacher–Christ, but we will need to be trained. We need to be more like Christ our Teacher both in character as well as in mission. We are not yet there, but we are growing. We will always need humbleness to lead people to Christ. Notice below how the Apostle Paul instructed Timothy. We should follow this pattern.

> *And **the things** (Gospel) which you have heard from me in the presence of many witnesses, these entrust to faithful men, who will be able to teach others also. (2 Timothy 2:2)*

- 'The things' refers to the Gospel or main content of Jesus' teaching.
- In this verse Paul shares how he has taught others like Timothy.
- Timothy is to train 'faithful men.'
- These faithful men are to teach others.

This is the way the Gospel has touched our lives. It is the same way God's truth will go out to all the nations. We make disciples.

Parents are to teach their children. More mature Christians are expected to teach the younger.

> *And Jesus came up and spoke to them, saying, "All authority has been given to Me in heaven and on earth. Go therefore and make disciples of all the nations, baptizing them in the name of the Father and the Son and the Holy Spirit, teaching them to observe all that I commanded you; and lo, I am with you always, even to the end of the age" (Matthew 28:18-20).*

Reflection

Discipleship takes place in many settings. Last night my three-year-old clapped excitedly as our family of ten sang together at our evening family worship. We read and discussed a passage from Deuteronomy and then prayed. The smallest ones insisted on praying for the orphans in India and for a missionary family, besides other family needs. What have they already learned?

Applications

- If you are a true believer of Christ, make sure you are baptized.

- Ask your disciple trainer or mentor to help you disciple another.

Summary

A) When I purposely listen to God like Christ did, God speaks to me and helps me care for others.

B) I follow Christ by replacing the world's influence on me with obedience to God's truth.

C) As people disciple me, I am to train others.

Take Home Projects

Memory Section Isaiah 50:4

*The Lord GOD has given Me the tongue of **disciples**, That I may know how to sustain the weary one with a word. He awakens Me morning by morning, He awakens My ear to listen as a **disciple**. (Isaiah 50:4)*

· Focusing only on Christ

Some of us have been greatly affected by popular theories, music and world opinion. The clearer we identify that which has influenced our lives, the easier it is to see what Jesus says about that teaching and reject it if necessary. In your journal, write down those people and ideas which have greatly shaped you. Ask your mentor, elder or pastor what Jesus might say about such people, movements or ideas. Learn from Jesus.

· Morning by Morning

Our closeness with the Lord depends on the frequency we meet closely with God in Christ through the Holy Spirit. Establishing a daily morning time with Him is essential for healthy growth. Plan to spend at least 15 minutes with the Lord reading His Word, praying and listening.

Did He say anything? Try not to leave His presence without gaining one special insight from your time together with Him each day. Keep track by writing relevant thoughts down and remembering it throughout the day. Pray about that item.

#4 King ⬌ Kingdom

*Growing in love
for God and others!*

King and Kingdom

Extending God's glory

We are called to be loyal members of God's kingdom where Christ is king, and we are His people. We establish His kingdom by living out His love and obeying His commands. Our own preferences are second to the wishes of our glorious King Jesus whom we gladly worship.

Our New Home

Have you ever wished for a place where hatred and selfishness is replaced by kindness and love? This is the kingdom of God. Man-run governments and societies will always fail us, but what we genuinely seek is the Kingdom of God.

You might ask, "Where is the Kingdom of Christ?" We usually think of a kingdom as the extent of a monarch's rule–wherever he holds power. Emperor Chin for example unified China by his rule. Christ's kingdom extends the world over through those who obey Him. His kingdom, then, operates differently from the world's nations.

Christ the King

The church is God's kingdom

Jesus answered, *"My kingdom is not of this world. If My kingdom were of this world, then My servants would be fighting, that I might not be delivered up to the Jews; but as it is, My kingdom is not of this realm."* (John 18:36)

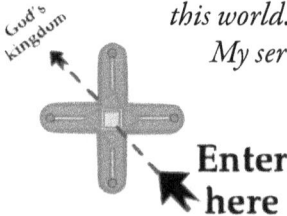

God's kingdom

Enter here

Complete the two sentences from the above verse:

"My kingdom is _____."

"My kingdom is _____."

God's people are His kingdom. His people are the ones through whom Christ rules through his command of love. *"He has made us to be a kingdom."* (Revelation 1:6)

Our Goals

A	God sent Christ to extend His kingdom ➡	Deliberately join in God's mission
B	Christ's kingdom is His people ➡	Purposely live by Christ's commands
C	We are princes in Christ's kingdom ➡	Properly respond to King Jesus in this world

A Participate in Christ's Mission
God sent Christ to extend His kingdom

God desired to extend the borders of His kingdom. He did this by sending His only Son, Jesus Christ the Messiah, on a mission to the earth. How did the Father accomplish this mission through Jesus? Jesus died on the cross to enable fallen man to enter into His kingdom.

1) Entering God's Kingdom

We cannot enter God's kingdom through our own efforts of being good or trying to help others. Instead we need to see our rebellious hearts and actions. It is then we ask God for forgiveness through Jesus.

This gospel message needs to be proclaimed all around the world. We see this is what Jesus and His disciples did.

> *To these He (Jesus) also presented Himself alive, after His suffering, by many convincing proofs, appearing to them over a period of forty days, and speaking of the things concerning the kingdom of God. (Acts 1:3)*

> *You became an example to all believers...for the word of the Lord has sounded forth from you... so that we have no need to say anything. (1 Thessalonians 1:7-8)*

Circle the 'kingdom of God.' By telling others of the king and the kingdom of God, people can know how to be part of His people.

2) Carry Out Christ's Commands

The teaching of the kingdom of God goes far beyond learning how to get into His kingdom. The Scriptures (Bible) also explain God's comprehensive plan on how we are to fit into it.

Although Christ could do a great job finishing this mission, the Father decided to complete it by involving His children. Each Christian is responsible to actively support God's plan to expand His kingdom of love into all the world. This is true of our neighborhood, town, country and other societies.

Notice how Jesus tells us to pray in Matthew 6:10, *"Thy kingdom come, Thy will be done on earth as it is in heaven."* We must take active steps to carry out the expansion of His kingdom. Telling others of the gospel is one significant way.

Application

1) Meaningfully pray Matthew 6:10 each day this week. Pause afterwards. Ask the Lord if there is a way you can do it that very day. Listen and watch to see if the Lord prompts you with any opportunities.

2) Ask God to bring someone that you can share the gospel with. Be attentive to whom the Lord brings into your path. Take up the opportunity!

B Carry Out Christ's Commands

Christ's kingdom are His people

Loyalty of Heart

Christ our ruler demands our complete loyalty. His kingdom consists not of land or material things but of the hearts of His people. When we become citizens of His kingdom, we have left the enemy's domain of darkness. We now belong to our King of love, whom we want to serve. Circle the word 'transferred' below.

For He delivered us from the domain of darkness, and transferred us to the kingdom of His beloved Son. (Colossians 1:13)

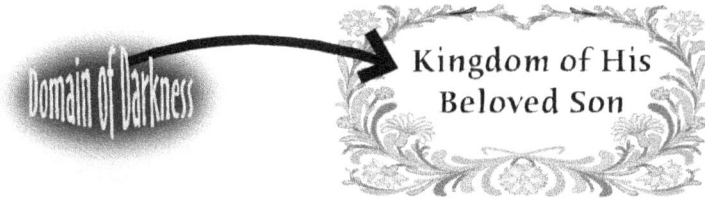

1) Loyalty of Life

Notice that as Christians we are now effectively members of Christ's kingdom. We are responsible to carry out His laws. The apostle states, *"So that you may walk in a manner worthy of the God who calls you into His own kingdom and glory"* (1 Thessalonians 2:12).

How should a Christian walk?_____

_____

Some people bluff themselves. They say they are part of God's kingdom but they are still ruled by the powers of darkness. One can observe their hearts by their actions.

For this you know with certainty, that no immoral or impure person or covetous man, who is an idolater, has an inheritance in the kingdom of Christ and God. (Ephesians 5:5)

2) Loyalty Forever

We need to be careful to obey the Lord. In this way we will prove that we really have entered His kingdom. As we sincerely follow Him, He will safely bring us to His heavenly kingdom.

The Lord will deliver me from every evil deed, and will bring me safely to His heavenly kingdom; to Him be the glory forever and ever. Amen. (2 Timothy 4:18)

The fullness of His kingdom will not appear until Christ is revealed in His full glory at His second coming. Then all His people will receive a glorified resurrected body and live with our Lord forever. On His robe and on His thigh He has a name written, *"King of Kings, and Lord of Lords"* (Revelation 19:16).

Application

Say a prayer committing yourself to follow Him all your life. You can use the prayer below if desired.

"Dear Father, thank you for delivering me from evil and bringing me into your eternal kingdom. I want to live for none but You. Help me to walk in a way that glorifies your wonderful Name wherever I am. I now commit myself to follow you forever. Keep me close to You. Protect me. I am looking forward to meeting you in your glory. In Christ's Glorious Name I pray, Amen."

C   Respond to King Jesus

We are princes in Christ's kingdom

1) Our Royal Relationship

The best picture of our relationship with our King is from 1 Peter 2:9,

> But you are A CHOSEN RACE, A royal PRIESTHOOD, A HOLY NATION, A PEOPLE FOR God's OWN POSSESSION, that you may proclaim the excellencies of Him who has called you out of darkness into His marvelous light.

Circle the word 'royal.' Royal stands for the kingly line or those things that belong to the king. We are not to expand His kingdom through guns and territorial aggression. We are His priests and therefore extend His kingdom by praying, living out and preaching God's Word. God's kingdom grows every time another person enters His kingdom. It grows as we carry out His ways.

2) Our Royal Responsibilities

Because of the character of Christ's kingdom, we can normally live in harmony with kings and governors on earth.

> ... I urge that prayers be made on behalf... for kings and all who are in authority, in order that we may lead a tranquil and quiet life in all godliness and dignity. (1 Timothy 2:1-2)

King of Kings

We are also to live in harmony with each other. If we all focus on the will of King Jesus, then we will not need to fight about 'our' this or 'my' that. *"If, however, you are fulfilling the royal law, according to the Scripture, You shall love your neighbor as yourself, you are doing well."* (James 2:8)

Instead we are to encourage one another to be faithful and loyal to each other. *"Not forsaking our own assembling together, as is the habit of some, but encouraging one another; and all the more, as you see the day drawing near"* (Hebrews 10:25).

In our assemblies, we are to express our delight in our King who has saved us from tyranny and brought us into His service. We are to be a thankful people who continually give praise to our great King.

> *You keep the commandment without stain...until the appearing of our Lord Jesus Christ, which He will bring about at the proper time-He who is the blessed and only Sovereign, the King of kings and Lord of lords; who alone possesses immortality and dwells in unapproachable light.... To Him be honor and eternal dominion! Amen. (1 Timothy 6:14-16)*

We worship the Lord with others each week. Psalm 100:2 says, "Serve the Lord with gladness; come before Him with joyful singing."

Application
• What is your attitude toward the world's government? Do you submit to the rules of paying taxes and obeying its laws?
• Tell the Lord three ways you really appreciate being part of His kingdom with all His other specially chosen people.

Summary

A. Eagerly participate in Christ's mission.

B. Know and carry out Christ's commands.

C. Properly respond to King Jesus in this world.

Take Home Projects

• Memory Verses Revelation 17:14

These will wage war against the Lamb, and the Lamb will overcome them, because He is Lord of lords and King of kings, and those who are with Him are the called and chosen and faithful.

• Entering His Kingdom

Our testimony should describe how the Lord called us into His kingdom. Write out your testimony in long and short form. Go over it until you can share it with others. Share it with one person.

• Praising the Lord

Sing at least one praise song to the Lord about His kingship each day this week. Learn to love to praise Him for His great love and power. Record the name of the song in your notebook.

• Finding a Good Church

If you haven't yet found a good church, you need to find one soon. A good church:

- Honors the Lord by encouraging obedience in His people.

- Loves to sings praises to God.

- Preaches salvation by faith in Christ alone. Evangelism is important.

- Provides small group opportunities to know and serve God's people.

This is not an ideal world nor are there ideal churches but use these standards to help you find a church where you can serve your great King.

Progress on projects should be recorded in a spiritual journal of some type.

#5 Bridegroom ⬌ Bride

Growing in love
for God and others!

BRIDEGROOM

BRIDE

Love and constant service

Bridegroom and Bride

Love and constant service

The wedding symbolizes the most inspiring commitment one can make in life. Christ uses the image of the Hebrew wedding not only to remind the Christian to keep purely devoted to Him but also to strengthen her patient longing for His return. Anything that would compromise her dedication to Him must be forsaken considering Christ's second return where the promises are fully realized.

The Hope of Love

We all need and long for love. A love that never ends. This is the reason weddings are such a momentous and joyous occasion. There is a romantic hope that a perfect love between two people will be sealed and protected for life. Up to that time, there is only the hope and expectation. The wedding secures that commitment. The engagement ring speaks of this hope but the wedding ring transfers those expectations into reality.

One moving part of the wedding ceremony occurs when the hand of the bride is placed into the bridegroom's. Her hope for the future transcends her fear of the new and unknown. She is placing her trust in her husband's future love and care for her.

The church as Christ's bride in a similar way is longing for the wedding day when all the hopes and promises become real. To secure her for her own, Christ paid a dowry. It cost Him His life, but He gave of Himself on the cross so she could be His own forever. Now He is preparing a place for her. Jesus says,

In My Father's house are many dwelling places; if it were not so, I would have told you; for I go to prepare a place for you. ... I will come again, and receive you to Myself; that where I am, there you may be also (John 14:2-3).

The Goals

A Affection for Christ the Bridegroom ⟹	Remain devoted to Christ	
B Christ's Soon Return ⟹	Focus on Christ's return	
C Keep Pure ⟹	Steps to a great marriage	

A Devotion to the Groom

Remain devoted to Christ

The Father arranged a bride for Christ the Son. Christ came and sacrificially secured that bride by laying down His life for her. The church is naturally called to be solely devoted to Jesus Christ who gave His life for her.

Affection for Christ

Marital commitment is two way. The groom desires, chooses and makes a lifelong commitment to the bride, his wife. She too is won by his attention and love. The bride responds to her husband by saying, *"I am my beloved's and my beloved is mine" (Song of Solomon 6:3).*

Just as a bride is given to her bridegroom, her husband, so has a Christian given himself to Christ when he became a Christian. This love for God and Christ is called our 'first love.' It can wear off just like in any romance. The Lord spoke against the church of Ephesus, *"You have left your first love" (Revelation 2:4).* We must respond to Christ's constant love by maintaining our loyalty to love Christ and His word.

Attentiveness to Christ and His Work

The devotion of a wife must always translate itself into attentiveness, the ability and willingness to tend to the needs of another.

> *Listen, O daughter, give attention and incline your ear; forget your people and your father's house; then the King will desire your beauty (Psalm 45:10-11).*

In the above verse, the bride is given four suggestions for maximizing her marriage. The first three were to call her to take the advice! Underline these three commands. The actual advice (the fourth item) told her to forget her father's house. She might get lonely or long for the 'good old days,' but then she would be focusing on her own needs rather than her husband's. Her responsibility now is to serve the needs of her new husband. Below, write down the result of what happens when the bride is rightly focused.

RESULT >_____

Reflection

A good Christian friend from another country once visited us during a barbecue with his Christian student group. He was one of the advisors. He asked me, "Why is it that so few people come around and volunteer to help?" There was no easy answer. There were a number of 'obvious' needs but no one asked if they could help. They were not focusing on the needs of others. He was just the opposite. He was very attentive to the needs of the church. Wherever there was a need, he would pitch in and help even at great sacrifice of sleep and time.

Application

Can you remember your zeal for the Lord when you first believed? Do you remember talking to others about Christ? Did you spend extra time in His Word? Didn't you joyfully go out of your way to help others?

What about now? Pray that the Lord would give you a love that surpasses how you loved Him in the past.

B Christ's Soon Return

Focus on Christ's return

The Hebrew Wedding

The Hebrew engagement and wedding was very unlike our weddings today. Once the man got engaged, he would go off and start arranging a place for them to live. She would not see him until he came to get her to bring her to their new home. This would be the wedding day. She never knew when he would come. She and others were held in suspense. She always had to be ready for him. When he came with all his friends, they would feast and he would take her to their new home. Read Jesus' parable (Matthew 25:1-13).

> *The kingdom of heaven will be comparable to ten virgins, who took their lamps, and went out to meet the bridegroom. And five of them were foolish, and five were prudent. For when the foolish took their lamps, they took no oil with them, but the prudent took oil in flasks along with their lamps. Now while the bridegroom was delaying, they all got drowsy and began to sleep. But at midnight there was a shout, 'Behold, the bridegroom! Come out to meet him.' Then all those virgins rose, and trimmed their lamps. And the foolish said to the prudent, 'Give us some of your oil, for our lamps are going out.' But the prudent answered, saying, 'No, there will not be enough for us and you too; go instead to the dealers and buy some for yourselves.'*

And while they were going away to make the purchase, the bridegroom came, and those who were ready went in with him to the wedding feast; and the door was shut. And later the other virgins also came, saying, 'Lord, lord, open up for us.' But he answered and said, 'Truly I say to you, I do not know you.' Be on the alert then, for you do not know the day nor the hour.

Alert & Perseverance

The point of the above parable is clear. The bridegroom stands for Christ and His final return to take His church, the bride, home with Him. The virgins represent the professing people of God. Some of them were ready for the Bridegroom; others were not. The consequences were serious. Even though the virgins might have been ready and eager at the beginning of the wait for the bridegroom, they needed to be ready for him when he returned.

We do not know when Christ will return. When He does, that will be the end of things as we know them. Because we do not know when He is coming, then it is easy to be distracted with other less important affairs of this life. As in the Hebrew wedding, the bride had to be busy, be ready every day for his coming for she simply did not know when her man was coming for her.

Application

List two things that you would not be doing (but are) if Christ came today and two things you would do (but are not).

If Christ returned today,

- I would not be doing:

- I would be doing:

Keeping Pure

Prerequisites to having a great marriage

Purity during marriage is largely determined by purity before marriage. If compromises occur before the wedding, only with concerted effort will they be prevented after the wedding. Every effort must be made to keep sexually and morally pure so that a stable foundation for a loving relationship can be laid rather than one that is ruled by lust. Genuine love demands purity.

1) Before Marriage

Singles must stay pure both sexually and emotionally before marriage. After marriage, their sexual expression will rigorously stay within the confines of marriage. Any compromise of these standards leads to deep marital problems. A bride must keep herself for her groom. A man must only set his affection upon his wife.

> *But do not let immorality or any impurity or greed even be named among you, as is proper among saints (Ephesians 5:3).*

2) Courtship and dating

To maintain pure standards, it is important to discuss them. This is hard to do in a dating context. Dating leads to an unsupervised 'fun' mentality with those of the opposite gender. This is especially true in a rich and mobile society. "*Now flee from youthful lusts, and pursue righteousness, faith, love and peace, with those who call on the Lord from a pure heart*" (2 Tim. 2:22).

Courtship, however, is a long term relationship that has marriage in view. Parents, along with the couple, give permission for the relationship to develop under clearly established standards. An accountability system is initiated by the father.

Courtships allow the couple to be together in public situations such as parks, malls and restaurants. They are not allowed to be alone together in private. After this trial time, the couple, with the parents' blessing can get engaged to be married.

3) Establishing Standards

What standards should a couple have before marriage? We suggest focusing on the inward (what a person thinks and imagines) and outwards standards (what one does with his body or words).

No matter what we do, we must stay away from sensual entertainment, suggestive pictures and intimate contact. Different cultures might have varying standards but at a minimum we suggest restraint on physical contact such as kissing or touching each other. Let the wedding signify the permission for intimacy.

PURITY
Courtship   Engagement   Marriage

Men are strongly controlled by sight while woman by the need for relationship. Clear standards help each one in his or her weakness so that they can keep each other accountable.

Application

Strive for moral purity. Strong rules help focus on the development of a genuine relationship. If you have compromised in this area, confess your sin, establish clear boundaries and make purity one goal for your life. A Christian, for example, should never develop such a relationship with a non-Christian.

> *"Do not be bound together with unbelievers; for what partnership have righteous and lawlessness, or what fellowship has light with darkness? Or what harmony has Christ with Belial, or what has a believer in common with an unbeliever?" (2 Corinthians 6:14-15).*

Summary

A. The Lord deserves my full-hearted service.

B. I will regularly ponder and delight myself in the Lord's soon return.

C. I will be sexually pure, both in thought and deed, in and out of marriage.

Take Home Projects

- **Memory Verses**   **Revelation 19:7-8**

Let us rejoice and be glad and give the glory to Him, for the marriage of the Lamb has come and His bride has made herself ready. And it was given to her to clothe herself in fine linen, bright and clean; for the fine linen is the righteous acts of the saints.

• Test of Readiness

Only some virgins were ready for Christ's return. What things do you need to work on so that you are 'ready' for His return? Write in your spiritual journal one or two things in each main area of life that you need to be doing to help confirm your readiness for His coming. Here are some categories you can reflect upon.

Work	Home	Studies	Relationships	Service	With God

• Project Purity

There are several different aspects to being pure. To be pure, there must be set standards. Those standards should be clearly defined. They should be of such purity that one is openly able to share them with others. Whether you are married or not, write down in your spiritual journal those inward and outward standards that God would want for you. For example a man should not be alone with a woman in a home. Find at least two friends and discuss what standards they maintain and why.

These standards should be openly discussed with ones partner and his or her parents. The man should make himself accountable to the parents.

Lastly, if there have been compromises in thought or deed, confess these sins, find cleansing through Christ's blood and a new commitment to those standards. *"Let the wicked forsake his way, and the unrighteous man his thoughts; and let him return to the Lord, and He will have compassion on him" (Isaiah 55:7).*

#6 Judge ⬌ Sinners

*Growing in love
for God and others!*

Judge and Sinners

Living in a Just World

The Lord God is Judge of the world. He brings judgment upon all who do not fully follow His laws. But who is perfect? No one. It is exactly at this point that God's great and mighty love reaches out to fallen, sinful man. In God's great mercy He sent His only begotten Son to die for us on the cross. Those who believe in Christ are freely pardoned. We as His people are to freely pass on this mercy to others.

Regarding the Rules

Recently, I was in traffic court. I experienced the extreme discomfort of standing before a judge. I had transgressed the law. Although I didn't purposely break the law, it didn't make me any more innocent. Those that filled the courtroom were waiting for their turn to give a defense for their actions. They like myself did not know what the judge's final verdict would be.

God is a judge. It might not be popular to speak about God as 'The Judge,' but He considers it His important duty to exact perfect justice.

As a just God, He cannot overlook the sins of anyone. Every last sin, big and small, public or private, thought or deed, all must accompany us to the Great Judgment Seat of Christ. *"The Lord comes who will both bring to light the things hidden in the darkness and disclose the motive's of men's hearts"* (1 Corinthians 4:5).

We only can escape the "Guilty" verdict in the finished work of Christ Jesus on the cross. *"And you know that He appeared in order*

to take away sins; and in Him there is no sin" (1 John 3:5). Only in Jesus alone can we find mercy.

Our Goals

A	God the righteous	➡	All are guilty sinners
B	Wrath Unleashed	➡	Christ suffered judgment
C	Mercy abounds	➡	Be merciful to others

A God the Righteous

Appreciating God's Righteousness

1) Understanding Justice

Because of our guilt, we tend to distort justice by lowering the standards or lessening the penalty. For example, we think that God makes exceptions for 'not so bad' sins. Although we may think God will not judge certain things or just overlook some sins, He will carry out judgment according to His standards on Judgment Day. In fact, God is responsible to exact a perfect justice. Every sin must be judged.

2) Good works

It is God's perfect holiness that demands perfect justice. *"God is light and in Him there is no darkness whatsoever"* (1 John 1:5). If God was a bit grey, we might be able to squeeze out enough good works to avoid God's holy stare, but God is all light. This means that unless we reach His perfect standard, we stand condemned. Underline the standard mentioned in the verse below and circle the true statement from the three following choices:

"For all have sinned and fall short of the glory of God" (Romans 3:23).

No one is guilty | Some are guilty | Everyone is guilty

The practice of doing good, like giving to the poor and helping people is excellent, but that doesn't take away our guilt for our sin. Besides, we have failed to do many good works. This is why those who trust religion, morality or charity to get them to heaven are gravely mistaken.

3) Our unrighteousness

If we are going to get to know God, it is imperative that we understand His righteousness as much as His love. God created man to live in perfect harmony with God's thoughts and ways. When man chose to reject God's ways, he went his own way. This is called transgression or sin. Mankind is unrighteous in two ways:

(1) He does what he shouldn't.
(2) He doesn't do what he should.

God declares our situation so bad that, *"All of us have become like one who is unclean, and all our righteous deeds are like a filthy garment"* (Isaiah 64:6).

4) A Rebellious Heart

At the heart of our unrighteousness is our stubborn and rebellious hearts. When a person does things that displease God, it reveals that his heart is defiled. *"There is no one who calls on Thy name, who arouses himself to take hold of Thee"* (Isaiah 64:7). This is why true salvation comes through the door of repentance. Unless we have a new heart, we will not have a genuine love for the things of God.

Application

Humble yourself before God and admit your guilt. You have fallen far from Him. You might take pride of some 'good works' but your life reveals how unrighteous you are. You deserve judgment before God's righteous throne. Confess your unworthiness to receive His goodness.

B   Wrath Released

Rightly responding to God

1) Questions about God's Wrath

God's wrath is an intense anger against all forms of rebellion against His person and ways. The word depicts the very way God will aggressively carry out justice. He will not lighten the sentence.

Our minds are so boggled with questions about God's judgment that we sometimes wonder whether God is really like that. The scriptures enable us to discover what God really is like. *"For the wrath of God is revealed from heaven against all ungodliness and unrighteousness of men"* (Romans 1:18). In a sense, it doesn't even matter whether we like the way He is. God pours out His wrath on the wicked; we should learn to accept this characteristic about Him. He openly has spoken about His judgment upon the world.

• Is God of the Old Testament the same as the God of New Testament?

Some wonder whether God is really as wrathful as the Old Testament states. The problem is easily solved by reading the New Testament. There we discover that God's wrath and judgment is described throughout the New Testament (37 times) just like the Old (147 times). *"He who believes in the Son has eternal life; but he who does not obey the Son shall not see life, but the wrath of God abides on him"* (John 3:36).

God's wrath is on all sinners already. Even without a chance to reject Christ, the curse of death clearly demonstrates judgment is already upon mankind.

• Can a loving God judge sinners?

Many people are certain of God's love, but they question whether love is compatible with judgment. They say, "If God is loving, then He wouldn't judge anyone," or "Since God is loving, He will save everyone."

God's great anger against sinners, however, is compatible with His love. *"Behold then the kindness and severity of God; to those who fell, severity, but to you, God's kindness"* (Romans 11:22). Underline the two characteristics of God shown in this verse.

2) God's Kindness and Severity

Terrible events occurring across the globe are genuine warnings to humankind. God calls people to repent and escape His soon-coming intense wrath. The Lord graciously warns us of His judgment through earthquakes, tsunamis and diseases such as AIDs. Suffering on earth is temporary, but His judgment has eternal consequences.

> *Dealing out retribution to those who do not know God and to those who do not obey the gospel of our Lord Jesus. And these will pay the penalty of eternal destruction... (2 Thessalonians 1:8-9).*

God's kindness is also found in the great sacrifice of His Son Christ Jesus. The innocent died for the guilty that the guilty would go free from His judgment. *"Wait for his Son from heaven, whom He raised from the dead, that is Jesus, who delivers us from the wrath to come"* (1 Thessalonians 1:10).

Application

Have you repented from your sin? If you are not clear about this, turn now away from your sin and plead for forgiveness through Jesus. God will forgive you and grant you new life so that you will desire to live His ways.

C   **Mercy Abounds**

Living out God's mercy

1) Understanding God's mercy

If we don't appreciate God's wrath, that stems from His holiness, then we will not be able to grasp the crucial idea of mercy. This is the problem Jesus identified in the parable of 'The Unmerciful Servant.' Peter asked, *"How many times should a person forgive another?"* Jesus responded by saying, *'seventy times seven.'* Let's summarize this illustrative story in Matthew 18:21-35.

Jesus illustrated how impossible it is for a person who received mercy from God not to act mercifully to another. This one servant had a huge debt to a king, something like ten million US dollars. The Lord of the land felt compassion and forgave him, but that same person went out and started exacting every last penny from a fellow servant who owed him a few month's wages. He choked him and said, "Pay back what you owe!" He was unwilling to hear the poor man's plea for pity and sent him to prison to pay back the debt. When the enraged king found out, he said,

> *You wicked slave, I forgave you all that debt because you entreated me. Should you not also have had mercy on your fellow slave, even as I had mercy on you? And his lord, moved with anger, handed him over to the torturers until he should repay all that was owed him. So shall My heavenly Father also do to you, if each of you does not forgive his brother from your heart (Matthew 18:32-35).*

Receive mercy ➤ 👤👤 ➤ Be merciful

Underline what God will do to us if we do not forgive others from our hearts. By withholding mercy, we shut off mercy from flowing into our lives.

2) Mercy is a way of life

Mercy is the willingness to treat a person in view of his weakness. The merciful person acts with compassion. He holds no grudges. He harbors no bitterness. He knows how special it was for God to kindly treat him by forgiving him and so determines to act kindly to others.

Reflection

Our perspective greatly shapes our attitudes. When God converted me, he revealed my sin to me. Before, I was oblivious to it. I knew I was not perfect, but I was

> **Seized by his own unworthiness, he reaches out to others with compassion.**

convinced that I was not too bad either. My point of comparison was my brother, "I wasn't as bad as ...." I simply did not evaluate myself according to God's standards. When He revealed my sin to me, I became totally desperate in a matter of seconds. I pleaded for God to save me through Jesus and He saved me. By being truly aware of my sin, I was then able to learn to be merciful to others. My pride was destroyed, and I could see others in my own circumstances.

Application

State the last time you acted mercifully? Determine to start acting mercifully. Start with those closest to you.

Summary

A. Because God is wholly righteous, our unrighteousness is very apparent.

B. God's righteousness demands that His wrath come against all sin bringing eternal judgment to those who are not in Christ.

C. We must be merciful as our Heavenly Father is merciful.

Take Home Projects

• Memory Verses Luke 6:35-36

But love your enemies, and do good, and lend, expecting nothing in return; and your reward will be great, and you will be sons of the Most High; for He Himself is kind to ungrateful and evil men. Be merciful, just as your Father is merciful.

• Honoring God's Righteousness

Read Revelation 14:17-18:4 aloud. Then write out a prayer in your spiritual journal praising Him. Praise God for His righteousness and that He is going to judge all sin. If you note a difficulty doing this, you need to first confess your blindness to God's majestic ways and seek forgiveness. Do this each day this week until it becomes natural.

• Monitoring our Mercifulness

When relationships get tense, check out your level of mercy. Most likely you have been withholding mercy. When a person withholds mercy, then God shuts off His grace to his life. As a person develops extra patience and kindness, his own relationships get much better. Examine your relationships to see if you have withheld mercy. Remember that mercy does not demand that another first take action such as in asking for apology.

• Pray for the lost

In response to God's mercy in your own life, ask God to give you a people group who are lost in their sins to pray for. It might be a home, street, city or nation. Journal His training of you to pray for this people group. Persist in prayer. It is a way you can bring more mercy into this world that deserves so much judgment.

#7 Priest ⬌ People

Growing in love
for God and others!

Priest and People

Learning compassionate prayer

The priest is an ancient and important idea found in every society. The priest's role is to be a mediator between God and man. We are not much surprised that Jesus Christ Himself is the greatest and most compassionate of priests, but perhaps we are surprised to discover that every Christian is part of the priesthood of believers.

Not Without Help

Have you ever felt vulnerable and alone with no one to help? If so, you need a priest. A priest helps us by standing up for us. He does what we can't do for ourselves so that we can get through our difficulty.

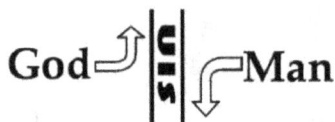

God ⮫ |S I N| ⮧ Man

As Christians, Jesus Christ is our wonderful priest. As priest He stands as a mediator between God and His people. Before we were Christians, sin stood between God and us. We lived in rebellion against God's rules for living. It was our state rather than one or two things we did. This was the way we were and neither could we change on our own.

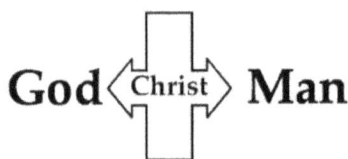

God ⟨Christ⟩ Man

We certainly did not deserve a chance to restore our relationship with God, but God in His great patient and kindness sent Jesus Christ, His only begotten Son, to die for us sinners. *"For there is one God, and one mediator also between God and men, the man Christ Jesus"* (1 Timothy 2:5).

We have lots to learn from the way God chose to reach out to us in our need. We will not only learn about how Jesus helped us get rid of sin but also how He wants to use our lives to reach other needy people. Try drawing each of the diagrams above.

Our Goals

A	God sent Christ to serve as priest	➡	Learn to have God's compassion
B	Christ serves as our priest	➡	Learn how to rely on Christ
C	We serve as priests to others	➡	Learn to care and pray for others

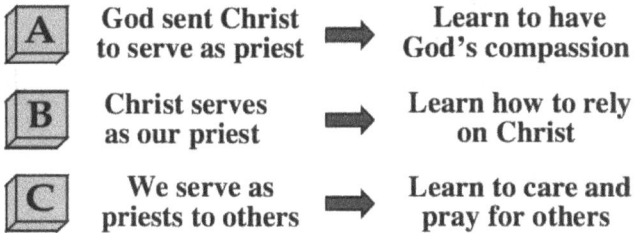

A **Being Compassionate**

Christ served as priest before God

We needed a priest to help us. God didn't have to help us. We deserved judgment for our rebellious ways. He could have let us die in our sins, but He mercifully sent His Son Jesus Christ to be a priest on our behalf.

1) The Need for a Priest

"... He (Christ) Himself bore the sin of many, and interceded for the transgressors." (Isaiah 53:12)

What are the two things Jesus Christ did in the above verse?

1. He Himself _____.

2. (He)) _____ for the_____.

Jesus Christ bore the sin of all His people when He died on the cross. Notice the kind of people He interceded or prayed for. It was for sinners.

God showed mercy to sinners who didn't deserve it. So why wouldn't we show compassion on others when we ourselves had been shown compassion? Whenever we see this lack of mercy, we need to remind ourselves of God's great mercy for us and others. We need to be full of compassion. God's full anger upon sin will come on Judgment Day. Right now we are to busily help others escape His coming anger by proclaiming how God through Jesus Christ can deliver people out from their sins.

2) The Obedience Priest

"Although He was a Son, He learned obedience from the things which He suffered. And having been made perfect, He became to all those who obey Him the source of eternal salvation" (Hebrews 5:8-9).

Notice Christ's example. We deserved to suffer, but Jesus the Righteous One suffered for us. What horrible pain He bore! That is compassion. Christ endured those thorns, scourgings and even death so that we the sinners could have eternal life.

Sometimes those who share the Gospel with non-Christians or help people who are being oppressed are persecuted. Tell the Lord in a prayer that you want courage and strength to help show His love to others like Christ.

3) Our Response

"For God so loved the world, that He gave His only begotten Son, that whoever believes in Him should not perish, but have eternal life" (John 3:16).

From the above verse, we read how Christ Jesus as a gift was given to us. But not every one is equally benefitted. Underline the key word that emphasizes what applies Christ's sacrifice to our sins.

Application

Develop deep appreciation for God's love for you by thinking more about how He would love a sinner like you and I. Take time now to thank Him for His love

B   Relying on Christ

Christ serves us as our priest

Because Christ cares for us, we can learn to trust Him more. Let's see how He cares for us and comes to our aid.

1) Christ's Intervention and Intercession

We sometimes find ourselves in difficult situations, but in many cases we can figure a way out. At other times though, we really get into impossible situations! Let's see what happen to this group of people.

> So the people came to Moses and said, "We have sinned, because we have spoken against the LORD and you; intercede with the LORD, that He may remove the serpents from us." And Moses interceded for the people (Numbers 21:7).

Underline the problem the group above experienced. Circle what the Israelites did when they found themselves in real big trouble?

> Then the Lord said to Moses, "Make a fiery serpent, and set it on a standard; and it shall come about, that everyone who is bitten, when he looks at it, he shall live. And it came about, that if a serpent bit any man, when he looked to the bronze serpent, he lived" (Numbers 21:8-9).

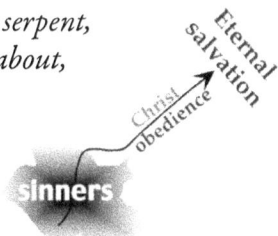

Eternal salvation

Christ obedience

sinners

The serpents were biting them, and they were dying. What did they need to do to escape the maddening problem. Write down God's solution.

John 3:14-16 tells us that this is a clear picture of how Christ can keep us from the cursed penalty of death. We only need to look upon Jesus Christ in hope. If we can rely on Jesus to deliver us from our sin, then we should trust Him to help us in other matters too. He has proved Himself as a very faithful priest.

2) Christ's Strength and Care

Christ Jesus is He who died, yes, rather who was raised, who is at the right hand of God, who also intercedes for us (Romans 8:34).

We sometimes might think that because Jesus died that He no longer has power to help us. This is wrong. The fact is that Christ who was dead is now alive! He was raised from the dead. Find out where Christ is and what He is doing by underlining the answer to the following two questions.

- Where is Christ Jesus now?
- What is Christ regularly doing for us who believe?

Application
- Let's review these teachings in your own life.
- Have you ever become deeply aware of your sins? Circle: Yes No
- Did you look at God's solution for your sin problem? Circle: Yes No
- Did you take God's advice? If so, when and where?

Caring for Others

We serve as priests to others

We understand that Christ is our priest but forget what the Lord has to say about our service as priests. We should recognize that this is not the same as Roman Catholics priests. Instead every Christian serves as a priest to the living Lord. God has appointed us to be part of His holy priesthood.

1) Our Calling as Christians

You also, as living stones, are being built up as a spiritual house for a holy priesthood, to offer up spiritual sacrifices acceptable to God through Jesus Christ. (1 Peter 2:5)

Circle three descriptions of God's people from above. This describes Christian leaders as well as all Christians including you. God calls His people to himself from the world and built us into a spiritual house. We are God's holy priesthood. What does 1 Peter 2:5 say our responsibility is as His priests?

"for a holy priesthood, to _____."

Three kinds of spiritual sacrifices that we Christians can offer to God are:

1. Share the Gospel with non-believers

2. Teach others about God's Word, and

3. Pray for others.

4. Can you add a fourth?

2) The Need for Action

And He saw that there was no man, And was astonished that there was no one to intercede; Then His own arm brought salvation to Him; And His righteousness upheld Him. (Isaiah 59:16)

Very few people genuinely care for others. An even much smaller number care and do something about it! We, however, are to follow in Christ's footsteps. We are not only to have compassion for people but also to intercede for them. Intercession is a fancy way to say praying for others.

We as God's people need to care for others as God has cared for us. As He prays for us, we are to pray for other Christians and the salvation of those who do not know Him. To be an intercessor, we need to:

(1) Be clean: Harbor no unconfessed sin and live uprightly.

(2) Be confident: Believe God can mightily wants to use your prayers.

(3) Be compassionate: Care about those around you. Be attentive to their needs.

Reflection

A cell group leader once told me that he was very discouraged. Things were not going well in the group. At one point he was very eager and prayed a lot for the individuals, but as the situation deteriorated, he prayed less and less. His faith dribbled away. Then a leader exhorted him to get up early to pray like he had at first if that's what it took to meet God. So the next morning, he got up early and had a good time in the Word. God encouraged him to continue. Interestingly, that night's cell group went extremely well. He again is back to fervently praying for the group. We must pray in faith even in difficult circumstances.

Application

Mention two particular individuals or groups that need special prayer. Pray together for them.

Summary

A. God showed compassion by sending Christ to die on the cross for us.

B. The more we trust Christ, the more secure we become.

C. God wants us to represent Him on earth by having compassion on the needy and praying for them.

Take Home Projects

· Memory Verses 1 Peter 2:9-10

But you are a chosen race, a royal priesthood, a holy nation, a people for God's own possession, that you may proclaim the excellencies of Him who has called you out of darkness into His marvelous light for you once were not a people, but now you are the people of God; you had not received mercy, but now you have received mercy.

· Develop a prayerful attentiveness

Each day this week ask God to reveal to you the needs of those around you. God uses all sorts of means to reveal things to us such as circumstances, phone calls, news, Bible readings, etc. Record them and bring the list next week. Say a prayer for each of these needs and follow up any concrete way God leads.

· Develop an evangelism lifestyle

Learning compassion and helping people is fine, but we must remember that without hearing the Gospel of Jesus, people will still perish.

(1) Review your testimony on how God saved you.

(2) Go over the Gospel using the chart earlier on (or another).

(3) Ask God for an opportunity to share the Gospel with one person.

(4) Tell the Gospel to this one person this week if possible.

(5) Share your experience with someone.

By evangelism lifestyle, you should always be sensitive with whom the Lord would prompt you to share His Gospel.

#8 Master ◆➤ Servant

Growing in love
for God and others!

Master and Servant

Devotedly serving God and others

Adam and Eve resisted God's rightful ownership almost from the start. We find that we still have the same problem–we want no master. Fortunately, our very patient Lord sent Jesus to show that being God's servant is not bad at all. Everyone is a slave to someone. The key, Jesus explains, is to serve a good master and trust His will to be the best thing for you. It sounds risky but it isn't considering your Master is also the One that designed and greatly loves you.

Follow the Leader

Many people gauge success by how many people are 'under' them, that is, by how many people work for them. The world looks up to these business leaders. Jesus shook the world's assumptions by declaring that fulfillment in life comes through serving others rather than being served. In the spirit of God's love, Christ, the Servant Leader, perfectly modeled excellent service.

For whoever wishes to save his life shall lose it, but whoever loses his life for My sake, he is the one who will save it (Luke 9:24).

Jesus served well. A master or boss gives commands, sets the agenda and tells his workers how to fulfill his directions. Jesus Christ discerned His Father's will, denied His personal preferences and purposed to do what was asked of Him. Jesus as a good servant was rewarded for His rigorous labor.

Therefore also God highly exalted Him, and bestowed on Him the name which above ever name ... to the glory of God the Father (Philippians 2:9-11)

A servant seeks to please his master. To properly fulfill his master's needs and wishes, the slave must give up all his own rights and purposes.

Our Goals

A	Christ devotedly served the Father ➡	Be fully available to serve God
B	We are servants to Christ our Master ➡	Willingly obey Christ
C	We are to serve one another ➡	Be committed to practically serve others

---

A Available to serve God

Making ourselves totally available to serve

When we assert our personal rights, we have clashes with other people. The solution for this kind of conflict comes by following Jesus' own example of humble service. He deliberately gave up His own rights so He could serve.

1) Christ's Example of service

Perhaps no passage so clearly identifies Christ's willingness to make Himself totally available to God and others than Philippians 2:5-8.

Have this attitude in yourselves which was also in Christ Jesus, who, although He existed in the form of God, did not regard equality with God a thing to be grasped, but emptied Himself, taking the form of a bond-servant, and being made in the likeness of men. And being found in appearance as a man, He humbled Himself by becoming obedient to the point of death, even death on a cross.

Underline the kind of attitude that Christians are commanded to have in the above verses. Notice the three different stages of humbling that Jesus experienced so that He could effectively get God's work done. Jesus, who chose to serve, is our example.

2) God's Choice of Service

Jesus didn't come to do what He Himself wanted but to do His Father's will. We often try to get out of hard situations. We think we deserve better.

Form of God
↓
Form of servant
↓
Likeness of man
↓
Humbled to death

For I have come down from heaven, not to do My own will, but the will of Him who sent Me (John 6:38).

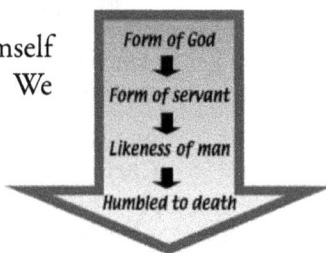

3) God's Means of Training His Servants

To make significant changes in our lifestyle, we first need to make fundamental attitude changes. Once we desire to serve someone, then we do not mind going out of our way to help him. The apostle in the above verses commands us to have the same approach to life as Jesus did.

4) God's Testing of His Servants

There is no doubt that some of our greatest temptations will be to give up when the going gets tough. Jesus faced extreme temptation at Gethsemane. Note how much Jesus' struggled. And yet, He persevered doing right!

Father, if Thou art willing, remove this cup from Me; yet not my will, but Thine to be done (Luke 22: 42).

Reflection

We were excited over our free tickets to the symphony. We later discovered that a special church service was scheduled for that night. I know my wife would be disappointed if we didn't go, but I knew what God wanted me to attend. I returned the tickets and trusted God for His special peace. We could serve together praying for others and trusted God to care for our needs.

Application
State the last time you were tested. How did you respond? Make a short prayer stating your willingness to always follow God's orders.

[B] Willingly Obey Christ
We are servants of Christ our Master

Jesus not only told His twelve disciples to follow Him but everyone who heard His message. Jesus is our Master; we are to do His will. Our faithfulness will be determined by how fully we obey His words.

If anyone serves Me, let him follow Me; and where I am, there shall My servant also be; if anyone serves Me, the Father will honor him (John 12:26).

Description of a Servant

In Jesus' day, a servant and a slave were the same thing. They were owned by the Master. The slave existed to do his master's will. The disciples never hesitated to do the will of the Lord Jesus. They asked Him questions, but they obeyed Him partially out of deference and partly out of trust. They believed Jesus would lead them in the right way and He always did.

2) Discerning your Master

We need to examine our own lives. Is Christ really our master? Do we really submit to Him? Jesus Himself told us that the one to whom we submit is our master.

Jesus answered them, "Truly, truly, I say to you, everyone who commits sin is the slave of sin" (John 8:34).

... By what a man is overcome, by this he is enslaved (2 Peter 2:19).

3) Deciding on One Master

Many of us struggle with someone being our master. So many seek our service or loyalty! A servant, however, cannot serve two or more masters. He must be loyal to one. Clearly identify any struggles and make your commitment clear.

No servant can serve two masters; for either he will hate the one, and love the other, or else he will hold to one, and despise the other. You cannot serve God and mammon (Luke 16:13).

4) Deliverance to Serve Christ alone!

Christ has set us free from complying to our selfish desires. The sinful nature that produces those desires is called the 'flesh' or 'old man.' Through faith in Christ, we are freed from ourselves to serve God instead. *"Even so consider yourselves to be dead to sin, but alive to God in Christ Jesus"* (Romans 6:11). The desires might be there, but we don't have to follow them.

Christ is our new master. We are no longer obligated to follow the flesh's desires. You might be tempted to lie, steal or follow sexual lusts. These desires are trying to claim your obedience. Instead focus on your obligation to follow Christ. Reject the feelings and thoughts of those desires. Set your mind on Christ through the Holy Spirit and your promised obligation to serve Him.

For the mind set on the flesh is death, but the mind set on the Spirit is life and peace (Romans 8:6).

Application

Are you aware of the tension created by your old desires trying to make you serve them? How did you respond to the last temptation you faced?

C **Practically serving others**

Serving others as Christ served

Christ had a lot to say about serving one another.

1) Christ's command to serve

Service is no option for His disciples. As Christ's disciples, we are to love one another. We are actually commanded to love our brothers and sisters. *"This I command you, that you love one another"* (John 15:17).

2) Christ's example of humble service

Jesus gave us an example of how He wants us to serve others.

You call Me Teacher and Lord; and you are right, for so I am. If I then, the Lord and the Teacher, washed your feet, you also ought to wash one another's feet. For I gave you an example that you also should do as I did to you. Truly, truly, I say to you, a slave is not greater than his master; neither is one who is sent greater than the one who sent him (John 13:13-16).

Underline the words master and slave in the verses above. What is Jesus commanding His disciples to do here? Circle your answer.

3) Leadership is characterized by service

Service is a special characteristic of those who are in any form of Christian leadership. Note Jesus' startling words.

And there arose also a dispute among them as to which one of them was regarded to be greatest. And He said to them, "The kings of the Gentiles lord it over them; and those who have authority over them are called 'Benefactors. But not so with you, but let him who is the greatest among you become as the youngest, and the leader as the servant. ... But I am among you as the one who serves (Luke 22:24-27).

• What were Jesus' disciples arguing about? _____

- Underline the two opposing forms of leadership in the passage above.

4) Faithful service brings great rewards

In the parable of the talents Jesus revealed God's delight in rewarding those who faithfully serve Him. A 'talent' is a large sum of money (eg. 100 pounds of sliver).

> *The one also who had received the two talents came up and said, 'Master, you entrusted to me two talents; see, I have gained two more talents.' His master said to him, 'Well done, good and faithful slave; you were faithful with a few things, I will put you in charge of many things; enter into the joy of your master' (Matthew 25:22-23).*

- How did the servant faithfully serve His Master? Circle your answer above.

Application

Reflect a moment on your attitude toward serving others. How do you joyfully serve others through the things that God has given you whether it be wealth, a home, strength, knowledge or natural talent?

Summary

A. We selflessly serve the Father as Christ did by making ourselves available to do what He wants.

B. We regularly and readily obey Jesus.

C. We joyfully and faithfully serve others.

Take Home Projects

• **Memory Verse: Philippians 2:5-7**

Have this attitude in yourselves which was also in Christ Jesus, who, although He existed in the form of God, did not regard equality with God a thing to be grasped, but emptied Himself, taking the form of a bond-servant, and being made in the likeness of men.

• **Find and Serve**

Do you notice needs of others and ask whether you can help them? This is the task of every Christian. Discover three special needs you could meet. Ask God to help you fulfill those needs and do what is required with a servant mindset.

• **Using your wealth to glorify God**

We are stewards of what the Lord has given to us including our knowledge, talents and wealth. Do you give to God's work (the church) each week? Christians should give at least ten percent (tithe) of his real income. This is obedience. Begin to consider how you can strategically invest your resources to advance His kingdom? For example, maybe this year you can plan to give 5% to missions. Add a bit each year!

• **Taking Christ to Work**

We all seem to have someone that asks us to do things. This might be your boss, parent or government official. Some of us proudly think that 'our way' is better than what we are being asked to do. When we do it our way, we often feel like we need to lie. Confess this as sin. Do all things the way you are directed. Combine this compliance with an 'I really want to be God's blessing to _____' attitude. Note the things you need to change in your spiritual journal along with the results.

#9 Redeemer ⟷ Chosen

*Growing in love
for God and others!*

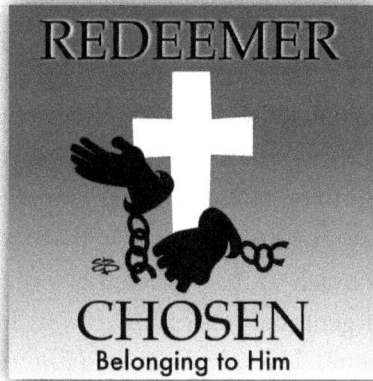

Redeemer and Chosen

God's design for me

Although this business term 'redeemer' (purchaser) seems impersonal, it plays an important part in strengthening our personal devotion to God. Once we comprehend what we are worth (nothing; deserving of judgment) and understand what God paid for us (Christ's life), our hearts are moved by His love. Humbled by His love, we respond by joyfully serving others for His glorious name's sake.

Desiring the Unwanted

Many people struggle with being unwanted. As the family structure deteriorates, self-hate grows. By experiencing rejection from busy parents, they question if they have any real value. Without love, they do not know how to love. They feel 'in the way.'

No matter how much we feel rejected by others, God's family is very different. God genuinely cares for us. His love is announced, proved and deliberate. *"He chose us in Him (Christ) before the foundation of the world, that we should be holy and blameless before Him"* (Ephesians 1:4).

God mentions His special choice of us throughout the scriptures. His choice for us reveals His special attention and favor. *"Yet on your fathers did the LORD set His affection to love them, and He chose their descendants after them, even you above all peoples..."* (Deuteronomy 10:15).

> Our value does not come from ourselves but upon what it cost to redeem us.

We know God loves us by the way He sent Jesus Christ, His One and only Son, to die and pay for our guilt. The righteous died for us the unrighteous. As we allow this truth to touch our hearts, we are greatly humbled and overwhelmed why God would choose us to be His forever.

Our Goals

A	God chose us ➡	Develop a deeper heart of gratitude
B	God bought us ➡	Endure suffering for others
C	We belong to Him ➡	Value one another

A

God Chose Us

Valuing His Undeserved Favor

1) The Need for God's Grace

We make purchases all the time. We might buy some vegetables or a book. Before buying an object, though, there is a point of selection. We must make a decision what we will buy. While looking over the product, we consider the quality, usefulness, and costs. In some cases we purchase the item.

Salvation is like this, but it has its differences. We had no inherent value of our own. Even though all of humankind was made in God's image, we had sinned against Him. The only thing that we really deserved from Him was to be judged. *"All of us like sheep have gone astray, each of us has turned to his own way"* (Isaiah 53:6). He later says, *"Your iniquities have made a separation between you and your God"* (Isaiah 59:2). A few good works or even many them is not going to eliminate our sins. No one is an exception. We all need God's grace.

2) Restraining Grace

The Lord shows a general love to all. He provides food and rain. Through governments and cultures He restrains our tendency to sin. Note how the Lord holds us back from sinning even more. *"Except the Lord of Hosts had left to us a posterity, we would have become as Sodom, and would have resembled Gommorrah"* (Romans 9:29). By God's grace we are not as bad as we would otherwise be.

3) Special Grace

The Lord in His marvelous kindness decided to rescue a great host of people from their sins. He would restore their relationship with Him. He did not have to do this. He chose to do this. This is the reason it is a dishonor to think that one deserves to be saved. Once it is deserved, then it is no longer grace but works, something worked for and earned.

"So then it does not not depend on the man who wills or the man who runs, but on God who has mercy" (Romans 9:16).

"You did not choose Me, but I chose you, and appointed you, that you should go and bear fruit" (John 15:16).

We are humbled by this truth. He chose us (elected us) in Christ not because we were better or greater but only because He wanted to bring His favor into our lives. We were selected. From eternity He chose us in Christ to be His own. *"And He did so in order that He might make known the riches of His glory upon vessels of mercy, which he prepared beforehand for glory"* (Romans 9:23).

Reflection

For over a year my sons would run up and down the streets looking under cars and behind trees for any empty can that others threw away. They treasured what others rejected. An elderly man would come by with his truck and collect all the gathered cans. The proceeds from the unwanted cans would help out medical research. God likewise chooses the rejected.

Application

We don't deserve to be chosen by God for His special work, but as His people we are. Quiet your heart and give thanks to God for choosing you to be His special child forever and ever.

B God Bought Us

Love's High Price

1) The Commitment

Decisions require a commitment. We can say, "I like that!" when talking about some piece of clothing in a store, but it is not the same as buying it. Some people 'window shop.' They only look at what is for sale rather than buying something. God in a generous mood could have said that He wanted to save us. That, however, is not the same as saving us. The Lord followed up His desire to save by committing Himself to do what was necessary to save us.

2) The Meaning of Redemption

The word 'redeem' and 'redemption' come from the meaning 'to buy.' In our case we were handed over to God's wrath and were under Satan's control. God redeemed (bought) us by Christ's blood, not with money or other things.

> *You were not redeemed with perishable things like silver or gold from your futile way of life inherited from your forefathers, but with precious blood, as of a lamb unblemished and spotless, the blood of Christ (1 Peter 1:18-19).*

The above word 'redeemed' was used when a slave was bought from another person. Ownership was transferred at an agreed cost. *"For He (Father) delivered us from the domain of darkness, and transferred us to the kingdom of His beloved Son, in whom we have redemption, the forgiveness of sins" (Colossians 1:13-14).*

3) The Purchase Price

Some people don't realize the reason Jesus had to suffer. They say they like Jesus' love but don't like the blood and gore of the cross. They go together, however, and cannot be separated. To carry out God's commitment to really save us from His own wrath, He sent Christ His Son to suffer and die to for us. The cross reminds us of God's real commitment to save His people.

The chastening for our well-being fell upon Him, and by His scourging we are healed..., the Lord has caused the iniquity of us all to fall on Him (Isaiah 53:5-6).

Underline the three times in the above verse where the transfer of penalty from us was taken by Christ. The iniquity and its judgment was ours. God can't overlook sin, but His justice does accept a substitute payment. That is, Christ paid our debt for us. He died for us.

> "You were bought
> with a price."
> 1 Corinthians 7:23

Because of sin, suffering is sometimes required to accomplish a greater good. This is what God did through Jesus Christ. Now with His resurrection we see the greater good come about in our forgiveness.

Application

Being able to accomplish God's will is more important than having a comfortable or easy life. God might even call us to suffer or be persecuted for His Name's sake. Tell the Lord that He is more important than your possessions and even your life.

C We Belong to Him

Expressing God's kindness to others

1) Working with Difficult People

We all have difficult times. Most of these hard times have to do with difficult people. Jesus, for example, suffered because of the jealous leaders around Him. God used His suffering to accomplish a greater good.

Christ trusted God that everything would work out just right. And it did. In the same way we need to trust God that our difficult circumstances are fully under His control. We have a lot to learn so that we can properly respond to these people. We must focus on being like Christ. Notice the attitude below.

Choosing rather to endure ill-treatment with the people of God, than to enjoy the passing pleasures of sin (Hebrews 11:25).

2) Responding right to Difficult people

When we rightly respond to difficult people, we communicate both God's wisdom and love. Poor responses are marked by anger, bitterness or jealousy. Instead of liberally showing them God's kindness, we hold their sin against them. Here are some ways to graciously treat others as God has treated us.

#1 Make a decision.
Decide to always treat people better than they deserve.

#2 Remember God's love.
God's love for you never stops. Even if other people poorly treat you, your value doesn't come from their actions toward you but from God's eternal kindness in Christ Jesus.

#3 Pray for your enemies.
Pray for your enemies. Never take revenge.

#4 Rejoice in God's wisdom.

Exert your trust in God by thanking Him on how he will specially care for you in such difficult times. You don't need lawsuits. You need Him to be your advocate.

#5 Make most of each opportunity.

Consider it your privilege to pass on God's love on in what would be otherwise a very evil situation.

#6 Don't budge.

Don't move from your commitment. It doesn't matter if it is your friend who betrays you or that you lose your house or job. Loving an enemy is a great miracle of God, and He has chosen you for the task. Do it well for His glory.

> *For what credit is there if, when you sin and are harshly treated, you endure it with patience? But if when you do what is right and suffer for it you patiently endure it, this finds favor with God. (1 Peter 2:20).*

Application

Make a decision to treat everyone better than they deserve. Consciously think and pray for those that might offend you such as your: spouse, child, parent, friend, colleague or crazy driver. You are going to replicate God's love towards you in Christ to those who don't deserve it.

Summary

A. I will always be grateful to the Lord for His choice for me.

B. I will do God's will no matter how difficult it is.

C. I have made a decision to be kind to others as God has been gracious to me even when it is hard.

Take Home Projects

• Memory Verses Colossians 1:13-14

For He (Father) delivered us from the domain of darkness, and transferred us to the kingdom of His beloved Son, in whom we have redemption, the forgiveness of sins.

• Deepen our Devotion

We are owned. We are esteemed precious. We can tell from the very price of God's Son Jesus Christ how much God loves us. We now belong to Him. Our hearts are filled with loyalty, love and duty. He has redeemed us to be His forever.

Set aside 15 minutes three times this week to meditate on this truth. Write down below when you will do this. You can use any verses that you know of to help you ponder on the God's love. Think about how special it is to be His and how undeserving you are to receive His grace. You have the option to write down your thoughts, but do find another person to share your thoughts with.

• Endure hardship

- List the hardest thing you had to do to be faithful to God. Did you do it? What was the result?
- Identify three difficult people or situations you now face in your daily lives in your spiritual journal.

#10 Cornerstone ⬌ Stones

*Growing in love
for God and others!*

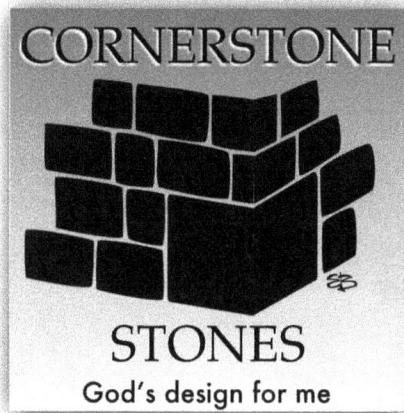

CORNERSTONE

STONES

God's design for me

Cornerstone and Stones

God's design for me

The Scriptures tell us Christ was chosen to be the key foundation or cornerstone to God's glorious spiritual building, His Temple. It is astonishing to discover that Christians are the 'living' stones that comprise this spiritual building. Our unique position speaks powerfully about how we are to relate to Christ and to other 'living' stones!

Built to Last

Jesus used many different symbols to describe Himself and His followers. The cornerstone is an architectural term. The cornerstone is the main foundation stone from which all other building blocks are measured and aligned. Christ is the cornerstone for the new spiritual temple that is being built.

Therefore thus says the Lord GOD, "Behold, I am laying in Zion a stone, a tested stone, A costly cornerstone for the foundation, firmly placed. He who believes in it will not be disturbed. (Isaiah 28:16)

The Jewish temple was destroyed in 70 AD. What is this new 'building' that has Christ as the cornerstone? God appointed Christ to be the first and most important 'stone' in His new 'temple,' the cornerstone. God positioned Him as the cornerstone of a specially designed building. Our hope is sure when we believe and follow Jesus Christ.

This new temple is the church, the people of God all built on Christ. We who believe in Christ are the figurative stones that compose this building together forming the glorious new Temple of God where God dwells.

For we are the temple of the living God' just as God said, I will dwell in them, and walk among them; And I will be their God, and they shall be My people (2 Corinthians 6:16).

Our Goals

A Christ embraced God's design ➡ Embrace God's design for my life

B Christ is our Cornerstone ➡ Focus on Jesus for effectiveness

C Christians are living stones ➡ Lovingly work with other

A Embrace God's Design

Christ embraced God's design as cornerstone

Christ's Example

Christ unquestionably embraced His Father's will for His life. He trusted God's design was best. He believed that all would work together to accomplish God's great salvation plan. *"And coming to Him as to a living stone, rejected by men, but choice and precious in the sight of God" (1 Peter 2:4).*

Circle the word in the above verse that states how people treated Jesus. Underline the words describing how God thought of Christ.

103

2) God's General Design

The cornerstone is the main foundation stone that every other stone is aligned with. To erect a marvelous building, it must have a trustworthy and solid foundation stone. The whole building depended upon it. We know the Lord not only chose the cornerstone but also selected each building block or stone to build the walls.

> *Christ Jesus Himself being the corner stone in whom the whole building, being fitted together is growing into a holy temple in the Lord; in whom you also are being built together into a dwelling of God in the Spirit (Ephesians 2:21-22).*

We as God's people are part of this 'temple' construction. Circle the three phrases that describe what is being built. To fit in, we need to accept how God has designed and made each one of us. Remember that our lives are designed with this final 'building' in mind.

3) Expansion of His Building

The Lord expands His building by saving people. Write down 2 passages that help explain this saving process.

4) God's Specific Design

Think through your own life. Are there any things that you would like to change about your life? Here are some that people want to change: background, physical features, socioeconomic standard, race, sex, nationality, other.

God wants you just the way you are! The 'unchangeables' are built into our life so that you can properly function well in His new Temple. There are things that we can and should change like our sinful thoughts and decisions. The unchangeables, however, must be accepted and embraced.

We are to rejoice in our wise God's design for our lives and serve Him just like Jesus did even if it means we are rejected by others.

Application

1) Underline any aspect mentioned above that you have wanted to change.

2) Confess your sin and ask for forgiveness by Christ.

3) Praise the Lord for making you just as you are! List at least 10 unchangeable things about yourself in the space below. Praise God for each of them.

B Focus on Jesus

Christ is now our cornerstone

1) The Foundation

Each building stone is fit into the whole building by its alignment to the cornerstone. Circle the word 'corner stone' below.

So then you are no longer strangers and aliens, but you are fellow-citizens with the saints, and are of God's household having been built upon the foundation of the apostles and prophets, Christ Jesus Himself being the corner stone. (Ephesians 2:19-20)

What makes up the foundation? _____

The foundational teachings of the church of God are established through the prophets from the Old Testament and the apostles from the New Testament. We must reject the teachings of those who differ with the scriptures because they reject not just the apostle's teaching but Christ's teaching as well.

2) The Distraction

One of the evil one's tactics is to get our eyes off Jesus the Cornerstone. Some Christian pastors and teachers will seek to please others. They speak the compliments people like to hear. Some focus on satisfying their pleasures. Paul gives us a caution on how we are to build.

Let each man be careful how he builds upon the foundation for no man can lay a foundation other than the one which is laid, which is Jesus Christ. ... Each man's work will become evident ... because it is to be revealed with fire. (1 Corinthians 3:10-13)

Everything will be judged by how well it complies to the Lord's building codes. The building materials must match the foundation, which is Christ. Think about your own life. Which area do you have the most problem with? Put a check mark next to it.

Pride: Trying to boost my ego by presenting a good image.

Jealousy: Wanting the attention another person is getting.

Envy: Desiring something that another has to look 'cool.'

Critical: Making ourselves look better than another.

We authenticate our faith when we look at and live by Jesus' standard. Peter once asked Jesus about John's future. Notice how Jesus' response pulls Peter back to focus on Him.

Jesus said to him, "If I want him to remain until I come, what is that to you? You follow Me" (John 21:22).

Application

Close this section with a prayer. Ask the Lord to give you a heart that always focuses on Christ Jesus. Confess your tendency to be distracted as noted by your check mark above. Commit that area of your life to the Lord and seek His deliverance.

C Teamwork & Love

Christians are living stones

1) Our Design

The Christian will never be able to get around having Christian 'neighbors.' God designed His building (temple) to be composed of Christians.

You also, as living stones, are being built up as a spiritual house for a holy priesthood, to offer up spiritual sacrifices acceptable to God through Jesus Christ (1 Peter 2:5).

Every Christian is a _____ stone. These stones are spiritually dynamic. They change their shape and grow as needed!

2) Our Relationships

This is what we find in daily life. As Christians, we need to continually make adjustments to our expectations and deepen our understanding of one another. We need to be careful not to get upset when a fellow Christian disagrees with us or does things differently. Circle the phrase below that Jesus uses twice.

A new commandment I give to you, that you love one another, even as I have loved you, that you also love one another (John 13:34).

3) Our Commitment

Love is the oil that keeps Christians caring for each other. God's love should deeply influence our own lives through two means:

PRAY

(1) Belief that other Christians are important and valuable. We find this true in the way that God has specially fitted them to be part of God's temple. They are also 'living' stones just like us. A stone wall with missing stones crumbles rather quickly.

(2) We are commended by Christ to "love one another." No matter what happens, whether we wrongly suffer loss or shame, we are still to love one another. Our commitment is shaped by God's love for us.

One other principle is important. Because we are not perfect, we are to master reconciliation. We need to learn how to straighten out a relationship that has deteriorated.

Reflection

I once shared a hotel room with a brother that was friendly enough, but we differed on how to carry out ministry. I could have pretended that everything was fine but that would have been deceitful. Instead I chose to love him. I purposely thought about him as a special member of God's body. I couldn't do without him. After prayerfully allowing these truths to touch my heart, I could really begin to care for his needs. The Lord led me to graciously share a few of my concerns. Other concerns I trusted into the Lord's hands.

Application
Think of one Christian you have difficulty with. Because he is also a living stone, begin to think of him (or her) as very important. Because of his importance, do everything you can to encourage and help him. Even go the extra step and praise God for that Christian.

Summary

A. I need to fully accept the way God made me.

B. All my decisions must please the Lord.

C. I must be committed to "love one another."

Take Home Projects

• **Memory Verses**   **2 Corinthians 6:16**
For we are the temple of the living God' just as God said, I will dwell in them, and walk among them; And I will be their God, and they shall be My people.

• **Project Reconciliation**
Think of one fellow Christian where your relationship needs improvement. Follow these steps.

1) In a prayerful spirit, detect if you have any fault.

2) If so, confess your fault to God. Overlook the other person's offenses.

3) Seek out an opportunity to apologize to that person.

- Confess your specific sin.

- Ask him to forgive you.

- If necessary make restitution.

Sometimes a person chooses not to forgive. You have done what is needed on your side. Keep praying for the person. Others mention their sins and ask for forgiveness. That becomes a special blessing. Give thanks.

We should keep going through this process until there are no missing apologies. Once done, all these issues move to the past. You can focus on building up your fellow living stones.

• Project Teamwork

Did you know that the term 'living stones' wonderfully depicts the biblical concept of teamwork? Each stone closely fits together forming a whole wall. Teamwork greatly adds to the effectiveness and joy of work just so:

(1) Someone clearly is in charge,

(2) The team members are committed, and

(3) The team members care for each other.

Think about your marriage, family, church, colleagues in light of this idea. Are there any ways that you could do better in your position? Make any necessary corrections.

#11 Husband ⬌ Wife

Growing in love
for God and others!

HUSBAND

WIFE

Faithful to my commitment

Husband and Wife

Faithful to my commitment

God has designed and ordained the husband and wife relationship. Hidden within this most intimate of relationships God also has given us a special picture of His relationship with His people. Oneness speaks of unconditional commitment, complete identification, whole affection and unending devotion. This also provides couples with extra motivation to continually choose to build one other up in speech, attitude and action.

Becoming One

A couple caught in the euphoric state of engagement has not yet come to the reality of what it is to live with another sinner. They live in the romanticism of their idealistic hopes. The realities of married life quickly settle in once the wedding is over. A few disagreements quickly subdue the glories of their special love. The disagreements don't mean that the couple has 'fallen out of love' as some might assume. Instead it calls them to focus on learning how to genuinely love each other.

Each spouse must learn to live by the rules for a good marriage. There are not very many, but they are important. The Lord even gave us special instructions on how to gain a great marriage, but the unseen foundation of a happy marriage is one basic truth. Marriage is based on an unconditional commitment. God declared "the two shall become one." They don't come apart.

Commitment is the willingness to stay faithful and be kind no matter what happens. Marriage is a 'for as long as you both shall live' commitment. That is the reason our Lord uses the marriage relationship to further our understanding of the intimacy He desires to have with His own people.

Our Goals

A	Christ is the Head of the church	→	Appreciate and respect my authorities
B	The church is Christ's bride	→	Develop trust in Christ and my husband
C	Remain faithful to each other	→	Strengthen my relationships

---

A   Christ is Head

Understand and appreciate authority

1) Understanding Headship and Authority

Authority is a very misunderstood topic. Let's first see what the Bible says about this matter. Fill in the blanks below from the verses below.

Lord

Husband

Wife

For the husband is the head of the wife, as Christ also is the head of the A, He Himself being the savior of the body (Ephesians 5:23).

Marriage within God's design.

_____ is the head of _____

_____ is the head of _____

113

The 'is' in the above sentences leaves no question to the fact of these two assertions. Can you without exception state this is so? Why or why not? Does a bad experience change these truths?

2) Crises with Authority

If you have seen hypocritical leaders, insincere husbands or just listen to the media, you might be one of the many people who strongly detest any form of authority. Along with this critical perspective is a strongly negative attitude that anything good can come from such an arrangement. Here are three challenges to confront and overcome to gain a great marriage or a good Christian experience in the modern context.

(1) Man believes he has a right to choose what he wants. He is 'in charge' of his own destiny. Humanism considers authority evil including the idea of headship in the context of Christianity or marriage.

(2) Modern man believes that he can change his mind about prior commitments as he sees fit. A person's changing viewpoint is more important than a vow. Divorce and remarriage become options.

(3) Submissiveness or compliance is considered a weakness and quite unable to sustain a person for normal living in the context of our modern world. It is looked at with disdain.

3) Our Hope: The Word of God

Because of the challenges to our faith, God has given us commands to direct us when we are confused and unsure about what is right. In particular, God has given a similar directive for both wives and the church.

> *Wives, be subject to your own husbands, as to the Lord. But as the church is subject to Christ, so also the wives ought to be to their husbands in everything (Ephesians 5:22,24).*

These commands for the church and wives are not optional. All Christians must submit to Christ's commands. All wives must subject themselves to their husbands. In the above verses, circle the phrase, "in everything."

114

Application

The need for a proper response demands a change in how we respond to the one in authority over us.

(1) Accept subjection as God's best. Plan to always obey.

(2) Confess bad behaviors and attitudes toward the one in authority over you.

B The Church as Wife

Developing trust in His irresistible leadership

1) The Commitment Questioned

Some Christians question whether Christ needs to be a person's Lord if He is their Savior. This is like the wife that reserves the option to not submit to her husband. Marriage is similar to our Christian faith in the way that the commitment seals how we respond to our spouse or the Lord. Underline the husband and wife's duties in the following verses.

This mystery is great; but I am speaking with reference to Christ and the church. Nevertheless let each individual among you also love his own wife even as himself; and let the wife see to it that she respect her husband (Ephesians 5:32-33).

2) Appreciating God's Design

Every time we depart from God's design, we run into all sorts of problems. We tend to assume our feelings or decisions are better than the Lord's, They never are. Have you been tempted to think that way? Probably. We all have. We need to resist those temptations. It helps to understand that God gives us commands to help and protect us.

- They remind us of God's way even when our experiences tell us differently.

- They arrange the relationship in such a way that there is no friction.

- They maximize the depth of joy.

- They protect the unity from threatening forces.

God's commands preserve and aid in obtaining the very best whether it be in a marriage or in our Christian life. Let's look at the reason for this.

3) Love Never Fails

Christ loves the church. His love is constant and sure. He is very involved with all aspects of our lives. We can trust Him during times of distress or confusion. We simply need to trust Him as the Spirit of Christ leads our lives. The husband is given this charge to unconditionally love his wife. The wife needs to rest in his care for her.

> *Husbands, love your wives, just as Christ also loved the church and gave Himself up for her... so husbands ought also to love their own wives as their own bodies (Ephesians 5:25, 28).*

The Christian and the wife both need to trust that all the love that is needed is always provided. As they do, their tempers and persons will be sweetly shaped to allow God's love to shine through their lives.

4) But if ...

Things are not always so easy for wives. What does Peter recommend? Underline the phrase starting with, "even if ..."

> *You wives, be submissive to your own husbands so that even if any of them are disobedient to the word, they may be won without a word by the behavior of their wives (1 Peter 3:1).*

Application

Thank God for your relationship with God and your spouse. Ask Him to build up your trust.

[C] Faithfulness & Charity

Living out our oneness

1) Working Out Your Oneness

Oneness, the indivisible unity in marriage, describes both the married couple as well as a Christian's relationship to Christ. Whether wading through some difficulties or just enriching your relationship, use this teaching to help you!

2) Never Two

Consequently they are no longer two, but one flesh. What therefore God has joined together, let no man separate (Matthew 19:6).

As much as we might sense a strain in our relationship, we need to refuse to accept it. This might sound a bit strange, but it is perfectly in line with what Jesus said. We affirm our oneness and refrain from doing anything that separates: negative criticism, hitting, yelling, name calling, blaming, etc.

Reflection

When a wife has a moody day, she can get critical and antagonistic. A husband can really feel the 'twoness' and can easily reflect that feeling by ignoring her need for constant love. Instead, remember your commitment to her. You don't feel like loving her but consciously decide that you will love her. You will choose to be more influenced by what is true–'the two are one.' Make a decision not to wound her but only provide your support and care for her as if she was you (she is) (Ephesians 5:28). It works. Anything less than this interferes with solving the real problem.

3) Pure and Faithful

Jesus' words *"every one who looks on a woman to lust for her has committed adultery with her already in his heart"* are well-known (Matthew 5:28). At times we will be tempted to be attracted to another person, especially when our marital relationship is experiencing rough times.

We need to affirm a life of purity. As a single, you train your mind to avoid its lustful path. If married, you remember your oneness and reject such wanton thoughts. Fix your mind on purity even if you need to first repent.

4) Kindness and Caring

God's commands help us affirm our oneness. *"Bearing with one another, and forgiving each other, whoever has a complaint against any one; just as the Lord forgave you, so also should you. And beyond all these things put on love..."* (Colossians 3:13-14).

We affirm our oneness when we refuse to act on upon those actions that separate us and deliberately decide to do those things that draw us closer together. Circle the actions below that affirm oneness between a married couple.

No divorce | Bitterness | Complaints | Yell | Listen

Prideful | Put up with one another | Critical

Patience | Stubborn | Love

Application

Choose two areas that you will work on. Accompany your decisions with concrete actions and prayer. See the take home project.

Summary

A. Authorities are God-ordained. I will accept and respect them.

B. I will always obey those in authority over me.

C. I affirm my oneness with my spouse by doing only those things that build up our relationship.

Take Home Projects

• Memory Verses   Colossians 3:13-14

Bearing with one another, and forgiving each other, whoever has a complaint against any one; just as the Lord forgave you, so also should you. And beyond all these things put on love, which is the perfect bond of unity (Colossians 3:13-14).

• Head & Toes

What do you do when someone in authority over you directs you to do something that you don't like? Write your response down in your spiritual journal. Do this for at least two situations. Be sure to include observations on your actions, words and attitudes. Discern whether your response was pleasing to the Lord. Pray, confess any sin and change your response to please Him.

Issue	Response	Good/ Not	Steps to improve
	Words	☐ ☐	
	Actions	☐ ☐	
	Attitudes	☐ ☐	

• Oneness Forever

From part 'C' pick out two things that will help you to affirm your marriage. If you are not married, that is fine, just do this with your relationship to the Lord. The same application works. Write down the two areas on the left and actual steps to take that affirm oneness.

(1)

(2)

#12 Vine ⬌ Branches

*Growing in love
for God and others!*

Vine and Branches

Abiding in Christ

The vine and the branches provides the clearest and most compelling picture of the abundant Christian life. Wonderful intimacy, constant devotion and abounding fruitfulness all spring from a close abiding relationship with the Lord Jesus. A good understanding of God's dealing with us considering His purpose transforms our whole approach to life.

An Abundant Life

Have you ever felt distant from God? Most of us have at one time or another. As God's children, He has provided a way for us to stay close to Him all the time. The analogy of the vine is one of the most illustrative pictures of our relationship with Jesus Christ and our Father. Jesus' words, enable us to better understand the intricate bond we have with God.

The branches draw their life from the vine. The outgrowth's constant dependence upon the vine is vital. The branches bear fruit only by being completely connected to the vine and allowing the life juices flow through them. This is a picture of God's people finding fulfillment in life by staying dependent upon God our Heavenly Father.

As we reflect upon this analogy, we will better understand why God cares for us the way He does. For example, our Christian lives might be dry because we have drifted away from close fellowship with Him. Many of our life problems can be resolved by purposely focusing on our dependence upon Jesus Christ the vine and enjoying His presence. This will be elaborated on below.

Our Goals

Remaining in Christ pleases God and produces more fruit.

A	God our Father is the gardener ➡	God carefully cares for His people
B	Christ is the vine ➡	God builds up ones life to produce more fruits
C	We are the branches ➡	Remaining close to the vine produces fruit

---

A   God is the Gardener

He carefully cares for the vine

1) God Cares for His People

I am the true vine, and my Father is the gardener (John 15:1).

God the Father is the planter and caretaker of the vine. The Father carefully prepares the soil to receive the vine and then when the season has come and the timing is right, he plants the vine. Carefully he cares for the vine, giving it what it needs and watching over it to bring it to the time of harvest. When the harvest comes, he gathers from his labors and delights in its fruits. God carefully cares for the needs of His people with the expectation that we will bear fruit.

2) God Deals with His People Differently

Every branch in Me that does not bear fruit, he lifts up, and every branch that bears fruit, he prunes it that it may bear more fruit (John 15:2).

What differentiates the two kinds of people in John 15:2? How does the gardener (the Father) treat each of these people?

1. _____   _____

2. _____   _____

3) God's Discipline of His Children

For those whom the Lord loves He disciplines.... It is for discipline that you endure; God deals with you as with as with sons; for what son is there whom his father does not discipline? (Hebrews 12:6-7)

'Lift up' refers to way a gardener will pick up the plant out of the mud to protect it from disease. In this Hebrew's passage there are three principles to help us better understand how God 'lifts us up' when we fail Him.

Fact #1. God loves you. God doesn't stop loving you when you sin.

Fact #2. God disciplines all believers when they sin.

Fact #3. God lovingly uses discipline to bring His people out of sin.

It is God's desire for you to be close to Him. He disciplines you so that you will return to Him. As we return to Him through confession, our intimacy with God is fully and immediately restored.

Application

• Identify any difficulties you are facing in your life.

• Observe if these problem might be related to disobedience.

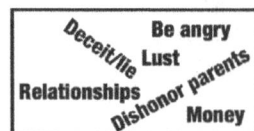

- Decide what needs to be done to change that decision.
- Confess your sin. Seek restoration in prayer, humility and love.
- Praise Him for reconnecting you to Himself.

B   Producing More Fruits

He prunes it that it may bear more fruit

1) The Goal: Producing Fruit

The branches of the vine must be pruned regularly or they will grow out of control and become entangled with other things which hinder the production of fruit. The branches must be constantly watched and cared for. The cutting or cleansing here that Jesus is talking about is the pruning or cutting back of the branches (John 15:1-11).

If there is no pruning, the branches can get so large and heavy that they are no longer productive. As Christians we can easily become comfortable and unconcerned about the production of any fruit, but God remains concerned.

2) The Process of Pruning

Pruning is an absolutely necessary step in order for more fruits to be harvested. Pruning serves several purposes:

* Removes diseased or dead branches.
* Ensures greater production.
* Eliminates wild growth.

Pruning is different from discipline. Pruning takes those who are abiding in Christ and makes them more productive by some significant difficulty or life challenge. Discipline, however, takes those not abiding in Christ through hard times so that they will repent and return to the Lord.

Self-examination 👀

God our Father prunes us when necessary, but we can avoid some trials by self-examination. Self-examination is that spiritual discipline by which we carefully examine what we are doing in our lives and taking initiative to make changes so that we can more effectively grow and bear fruit.

Application

If my grape branches pruned themselves, then I would not need to do any pruning! How can we work along with the Lord to improve things? Honestly answer the following questions.

- What might be draining your precious time and energy from what you are supposed to be doing?
- How might you ensure a more steady walk with the Lord?
- How can you better shield yourself from worldly temptations?

C Staying Close to the Vine
Abiding in Christ produces much fruit

1) Abiding in Christ

I am the vine; you are the branches. If a man remains in me and I in him, he will bear much fruit; apart from me you can do nothing (John 15:5).

To abide in Christ is to surrender your will and give Him your entire being: choosing to yield, obey, and receive all that He has for us. It is to become like little children, totally dependent upon Him for sustenance, protection, and guidance. Abiding does not produce immediate maturity nor does it produce immediate fruit. Rather it is the promise of becoming mature and bearing fruit ripe for the harvest.

2) Understanding His Promises

If you abide in Me, and My words abide in you, ask whatever you wish, and it shall be done for you (John 15:7).

Through abiding in Him, and His Word having its effect in us, Christ promised that we could ask anything according to His will and it will be done for us. Many take this promise for their own selfish purposes, never committing themselves to the abiding lifestyle. But those who follow its instruction will have what they ask, for they are full of the Word of God and ask in accordance to the Word that abides in them.

Reflection

Learning to trust God when teaching or doing evangelism has been a challenge. If I am self-confident, then I don't think I need Him. If, however, I feel inadequate, it is easy to worry about doing an inadequate job. I've slowly learned that the key is to always be consciously dependent upon Him. This starts when I realize that I cannot do anything good and will remains unless He is in it. I need Him. The sincerity of my prayer is dependent on how much I really believe that I need Him.

3) Chosen for a Purpose

You did not choose Me, but I chose you, and appointed you, that you should go and bear fruit, and that your fruit should remain, that whatever you ask of the Father in My name, He may give to you (John 15:16).

The better we understand God's purpose for us, the easier it is to cross over tough and confusing times. Notice here how God carefully chose us. He didn't make a bad choice. He chose us because He wanted us to experience His wonderful grace. He also chose to do special and great things through our lives. Although God might do great things through us to show God's love and power to the world, we are always humbled to remember that Christ the vine is the source of everything good. We are only His vessel (branch).

Application

Pray and thank the Lord for choosing you to carry out His mission. Affirm your willingness for Him to use you.

Summary

A. God carefully oversees our lives and will discipline us when we do not obey Him.

B. We will be pruned to produce more fruits. We need to trust Him during this difficult process.

C. When we stay close to Christ through obedience, Christ produces much fruit in us.

Take Home Projects

· Memory Verses John 15:4-5

"Remain in me, and I will remain in you. No branch can bear fruit by itself; it must remain in the vine. Neither can you bear fruit unless you remain in me. I am the vine; you are the branches. If a man remains in me and I in him, he will bear much fruit; apart from me you can do nothing."

· Develop intimacy with Christ

1) Keep a journal of your spiritual walk with God. Note the things in your life that keep you from abiding fully in Him. Ask God to remove these obstacles in your life one by one so that you can focus on worshipping Him. This is a spiritual discipline that we hope you start here and continue on to the end of your life.

2) Regularly thank Him and treasure His choice of you and all of God's people. You are special not because what you have done or will do but because He chose to work through you.

THE AMAZING GRACE OF GOD

Vine and Branches

Appendix #1 Objectives of Relational Discipleship

Growing in our relationship with God and people

To effectively transfer the essential relational truths of God to young Christian lives through the images of Christ and the church so that each Christian experiences the full potential of Spirit-filled living.

> Holiness:
> Loving God
> & others Christ's
> way

Problems:

Very few people are discipled. They are like babies that have not been cared for. Jesus has made it very clear that we should make disciples and not simply 'save souls.' Truly, God's people need to make disciples, but we also need to make good disciples. Just as one can be a good or bad parent, so one can be a good or bad discipler.

The discipling material that the few discipled people use is a good beginning, but it lacks training in critical areas. Would you like to be the child who is not trained to be polite to others?

Creating a new movement among the peoples of the world to be aware of how God is desiring to relate to them.

We are not trying to overload basic discipleship material with more content. A child learns things at different stages. The same is true with Christians. What is it then that is being neglected in these basic discipleship courses?

Chief Concern

Our chief concern is that every basic discipleship material focuses on man's relationship with God. This is good and needed, but they are missing another whole side of things–man's relationship with man.

This has resulted in Christians who seem to be promising leaders but in the end they fail the test of working well with others. Even more hazardous are those who slide into leadership without their lives being properly prepared. In either case their poor marriage or relationship with coworkers creates unnecessary tension and problems.

> *Truth always has its demand on our lives. In some cases we have already been shaped by His truth so we do not feel its effect. For example, those who grew up under the blessing of good marriages have already learned much about the truths that make up a great marriage.*

Jesus said that the summary of all the commands focuses on loving God and other people. We need to use the opportunity of basic discipleship training to train God's people both in their relationship with God and man. There are other significant side benefits from doing this.

Easy Learning	Sight Learning	Spiritual Learning
God has built truths and essential concepts right into our personal relationships.	These relationships such as father-son hold special ways to grasp spiritual truths.	Our deepening relationship with God through His Word sheds light on how we are to treat each another. (eg. Learn how to be a good father from God).

Means

To effectively transfer character qualities to our lives as seen in the chart below.

• Father – Son	Obedience, Loyalty
• Shepherd – Lamb	Provision, healing
• Teacher – Disciple	Teachable, wisdom
• King – Kingdom	Obedience, meek
• Bridegroom – Bride	Intimacy, affection
• Judge – Sinners	Righteousness, mercy
• Priest – People	Endurance, service
• Master – Servant	Faithful, attentive
• Redeemer – Chosen	Belonging, choice
• Cornerstone – Stones	Dependence, cooperation
• Husband – Wife	Covenant, obligation
• Vine – Branches	Dependence, fruit

Appendix #2 Relational Discipleship User's Guide

Relational Discipleship is a basic discipleship course.

This is in contrast to more specialized training that is found for other discipleship material. We suggest that it is used after a new believer's introduction to the Christian life. BFF has a 3 X E foundational basic discipleship booklet that helps the new believer (or one who hasn't been discipled) to possess a good overall grasp of basic Christian living and duties.

• Filling the gap

The *Relational Discipleship* series helps fill a big gap in the discipleship material that is now available. Most basic discipleship materials have two chief weaknesses.

They are self-focused. They ignore the church context in which each Christian is born and should be attached to. The reason for this is that it is non-church ministries that have chiefly developed discipleship materials, mostly student ministries. Most students have a great difficulty in becoming an active member in a local church.

They almost exclusively focus on a Christian's spiritual relationship with God. Of course this is what is new. Before they had no relationship with God and now they do. The problem is that when people learn things of God without associating these things with their relationships with others, that big gaps appear in their perspectives.

In either scenario, not to mention the even more severe lack of any discipleship training, problems in relating to other Christians develop. This course aims to integrate the development of both the spiritual (vertical) and the person-to-person (horizontal) relationships. If a Christian is to grow, he or she must understand this or they will be crippled from future growth. Read the *Relational Discipleship* introduction to learn more on how this material was designed.

- An overview of a lesson

The twelve lessons are most effective in a ninety-minute one-to-one mentor-discipleship situation. They can be used in small groups of two or three or even in a class. The larger the class, the less effective each lesson becomes due to the lack of personal application. This is unfortunately always true with training.

The study should generally follow the order below. If only sixty minutes is available, then skip one or two minor sections out of each main point and have them read it at home. If only twenty or thirty minutes can be arranged, then just do one or two goals at a time, just remember to introduce the theme and the three goals each time.

90 Minute Schedule

Cheerfully greet each other; have a brief conversation. Open with prayer.

- Review past lesson and the Take Home Project (10-15').
- Introduce the week's lesson. Hand them the booklet. Introduce theme, introduction and three goals. Emphasize what needs to be learned about God and relationship with others (10').
- Introduce Goal A and discuss. Do application together (20').
- Introduce Goal B and discuss. Do application together (20').
- Introduce Goal C and discuss. Do application together (20').
- Summarize and clarify the Take Home Projects (5').
- Close in prayer. Each person prays specifically about the lessons learned.

There are two ways to use this material.

• As a general topical guide

In this case the mentor does not closely follow the text. He will have the student read it at home once during the week. However, He does follow the general outline and touches upon the material that he wants to use including Bible verses, significant points and illustrations. When the trainee returns home, then the reading of the material and Take Home Project will reinforce what was earlier taught. Certain points will be chosen the next time to review.

• As a specific reading guide

Here the mentor closely follows the booklet. Large parts of it will be read together. The mentor can read a part and then ask the trainee to read a part. We would suggest that you state the introduction in your own words or develop your own personalized one. Once you read through a few lessons, then the lesson's basic structure will become noticeable. You will be able to better use the training tool (the booklet). This in turn will result in more 'teaching' freedom. Each mentor should work toward the goal of using the booklet to help facilitate conversation rather than dominate ones time. Meanwhile, discipleship is better done than neglected. Remember the booklets are designed to be read without a mentor so even if one does not 'finish' the material, that is fine. Assign it as home reading or just go a bit slower. Focus on the application points which are spread throughout the material.

• Use of the lesson material

We suggest that the teacher arrange for ordering or copying the instructional booklets and hand them out one by one as you meet. This has two advantages. First, the student has them with them. Second, they build up expectation by introducing the new coming material. Towards the end, one can give them the extra teacher material and discuss how you hope they can train another person. Perhaps volunteer to sit in a training time with another as they lead another person or have them sit in with you in another training class of yours. You can ask them to share a few things they learned in the past lessons! They get to share, inspire others and gain confidence to do it on their own.

Obtaining the Relational Discipleship resources

We welcome you to make copies of the booklets for your students. We realize that convenience and costs are important for some. Others will translate them. That is fine.

The *BFF Discipleship Training Library #1* has many advantages. Not only are various pdf formats available in color, but so are Relational Discipleship Power point slides and the teacher's instructional manual.1

Personalize the lesson as much as possible. Some people feel bound to 'go by the book.' We suggest you feel free to add your own illustrations, especially the personal ones from your own life. The more a person can personalize the lesson, the better it is. A disciple learns a lot from learning how his mentor had gone through learning situations.

Biblical. All our material is built from the Bible up! We are fully Bible-believing conservatives who believe that the Bible is not being believed enough in our lives. We want to train people to believe and live them out so that they see the power of Christ in their lives.

Have them read the actual Bible text aloud. The disciple should have his Bible ready to use even though most of the verses are included in the text (NASB). The disciple should find and read the verses in their own Bible to help them familiarize themselves with God's Word, especially if they are new to the Bible.

Individualize the lesson. The discipler must pay special attention to the needs of the person being discipled. This curriculum can be used to disciple people at different levels. Some have little background in the Bible while others understand a significant amount. The discipler must adjust his questions, speed and introduction of other materials as needed. If the material is too

---

1 http://www.foundationsforfreedom.net/Help/Store/Intros/BFF_D1_DVD.html

much for a session, spend a few sessions on it. Go according to the need of the trainee. The Cross Trainer Teacher's Guide provides extra resources for the mentor or discipler.

Sometimes there are fill-in-the-blank or other questions that elicit a reply. Patiently guide the trainee as needed into finding the answers. These 'mini-studies' are to help both the mentor and trainee. This gives the mentor an opportunity to show the trainee how to study. The student will through this be trained how to look in the Bible text for answers to simple straightforward questions. The questions are purposely kept very simple. They might be easy for you but they might not be for the trainee.

Clear organization. Each lesson has three goals introduced early on along with their purpose. This helps organize ones time together for both the trainer and trainee. One can give more time to one section or another but try to stay within the allotted time. Adjust discussion as needed. Skip a minor point or two. Just remember to discuss the three major points. If the student has already mastered one area, then one should be able to go on quicker, or have them share more of what they have learned or how they have learned such things. The mentor should feel bound to help the student reach those goals.

Too much to say! At times as a teacher many additional thoughts will come to your mind that you want to teach. You have so much to say! Carefully go back to the purposes of the lesson and choose the best thought or illustration that supports the purpose of the lesson or section of the lesson. You can take those additional verses, thoughts and even illustrations and put them in your own booklet. Either write your thoughts right into the margin or add another page and place it as an insert into your instruction booklet.

Training others to disciple.

Remember to encourage these trainees from the beginning to take good notes so that they can disciple others just like you are doing. You can ask the student to highlight, circle or underline certain words in their instruction booklet. It should become their copy that they can later use to help instruct others. Of course they will have many other thoughts right from their own spiritual journals.

Spiritual journaling.

Christians need to learn to reflect on their life events before the Lord. In our busy day, taking a leisurely stroll through the field is not common. So instead have them create a notebook (or computer document) that helps them reflect through their life. Encourage the student to do their assignments right in their spiritual journal. We hope that this will develop into a long-lasting spiritual discipline. Tell them this! They can write down prayers, special Bible passages, life-lessons, strong temptations, prayer requests, etc.

Take Home Projects.

It is important that the student does the studies listed. They can of course be adapted to the need of the trainee. However, they should be done. Time must be allocated to go over and see whether they memorized their verses and how the actual studies went. This is a discipling time. You need to be personal. Ask them, for example, which people did they need to forgive. Get specific! Don't be so polite that the studies become sterile. It is imperative that that the information is treated privately. These studies are designed to bring God's truth into their lives.

Learning to Pray.

Numerous assignments require the young believer to pray. Sometimes Christians might be reluctant to pray because they have never heard anyone pray before. Some churches unfortunately only have the pastor praying aloud. The mentor needs to gently lead them to pray. Start off small. Sometimes they just do not know how to start (Dear Father in Heaven) or stop (In Jesus Christ's Name we pray, Amen). If they are very reluctant, just have them repeat after you in short phrases.

Other resources.

Familiarize yourself with the other material on the BFF (www.foundationsforfreedom.net) website. If the person shows much initiative, have them go to the homepage and just type in the topic like abiding, vine or foundation. He or she will find many pages with great biblical instruction.

Questions and Answers

Q: Is the material appropriate for those who have been a Christian a while?

A: Sure. Many Christians have not learned the basics. The lessons are still needed though unfortunately late.

Q: I sense there is just so much to learn but so little time.

A: That is a great attitude for learning and teaching! Go through the booklets and then in a few years go through them again. At every stage in life, they become differently important. Remember the basic relationships in life are constantly instructing us.

Q: Can I use these materials on a brand new Christian?

A: You can. There is no harm. The basics are taught here but in a different framework. We do suggest that you go through a shorter most basic discipleship course first such as the one suggested above (3 X E).

Q: I feel that I am just learning so much. How can I disciple another?

A: No one is never fully ready to teach on their own. We need learn how to teach with the Holy Spirit. Extra confidence is as dangerous as the lack of confidence. We disciple because we are being obedient to Christ's command.

Q: What training materials can we use after *Relational Discipleship*?

A: Check out *The Life Core* which provides a clear understanding how and why believers spiritual grow.[2] This gives you a survey of the whole discipleship process and why training is so important in the local church. Each church should outline what goals they have for each stage of the Christian and then choose suitable materials to

---

[2] Please note that the BFF Discipleship Training Library #1 includes both *The Life Core* as well as the *3 X E Discipleship* booklet for new believers. www.foundationsforfreedom.net/Help/Store/Intros/Life_Core.html

train believers. We have resources on helping the believer to learn to read/study the Bible on their own as well as well as our second level discipleship resources which help move the young believer move to full maturity.[3] This second stage helps the believer know how to use God's Word to regularly overcome temptations and trust God in various life situations.

[3] www.foundationsforfreedom.net/Help/Store/Intros/BFF_D2_DVD.html

Appendix #3 Book Summary

Relational Discipleship is a basic discipleship course designed to develop a solid Biblical grounding for Christians in their early Christian walk. Ideally, this material should be led by a mentor. This twelve lessons are founded on Jesus' summary of all the commandments in Mark 12:30-31.

"And you shall love the Lord your God with all your heart, and with all your soul, and with all your mind. The second is this, 'You shall love your neighbor as yourself.' There is no other commandment greater than these."

The scriptures integrate our relationship with God with the relationships with other people. We cannot grow in our relationship with God more than we are willing and able to grow in our relationship with other people. The opposite is true too. We cannot grow in our relationship with others any quicker than we grow closer to God.

Benefits of Cross †raining

- Scripture models form the numerous themes
- Synthesize truths around the model
- Apply basic truths applicable to our growing relationship with God
- Apply basic truths applicable to growing relationship with people
- Deepen learning by merging both vertical and horizontal relationships
- Set a good foundation upon which new disciples understand God's glorious work in their whole lives.

- Can be used one-to-one, small group or in a teaching situation.

Appendix 4: Cross Trainer Bible References

* Memorized Verses

Key to titles

- #1 Father – Son (FS)
- #2 Shepherd – Lamb (SL)
- #3 Teacher – Disciple (TD)
- #4 King – Kingdom (KK)
- #5 Bridegroom – Bride (BB)
- #6 Judge – Sinners (JS)
- #7 Priest – People (PP)
- #8 Master – Servant (MS)
- #9 Redeemer – Chosen (RC)
- #10 Cornerstone – Stones (CS)
- #11 Husband – Wife (HW)
- #12 Vine – Branches (VB)

Old Testament

Numbers 21:7-9 (PP)
Deuteronomy 10:15 (RC)
Job 36:22 (TD)
Psalm 23:1-2,4 (SL)
Psalm 45:10-11 (BB)
Psalm 100:2 (KK)
Psalm 100:2-3 (SL)
Song of Solomon 6:30 (BB)
Isaiah 28:16 (CS)
*Isaiah 50:4 (TD)
Isaiah 53:5-6 (RC)
Isaiah 53:12 (PP)
Isaiah 55:7 (BB)
Isaiah 59:2 (RC)
Isaiah 59:16 (PP)
Isaiah 64:6-7 (JS)
Jeremiah 29:12-13 (SL)
Ezekiel 34:11-12 (SL)

New Testament

Matthew 3:17 (FS)
Matthew 5:7 (JS)
Matthew 5:9 (FS)
Matthew 5:16 (FS)
Matthew 5:28 (HW)
Matthew 5:44-45 (FS)
Matthew 6:10 (KK)
Matthew 7:11 (FS)
Matthew 10:16 (SL)
Matthew 18:21-35 (JS)
Matthew 19:6 (HW)
Matthew 25:1-13 (BB)
Matthew 25:22-23 (MS)
Matthew 26:52-53 (FS)
Matthew 28:18-20 (TD;SL)
Mark 1:22 (TD)
Mark 2:18 (TD)
Mark 6:34 (SL)
Mark 10:15 (KK)
Luke 2:46-47 (TD)
*Luke 6:35-36(JS)
Luke 6:40 (TD)
Luke 9:24 (MS)
Luke 16:13 (MS)
Luke 22:24-27 (MS)
Luke 22:42 (MS)
John 3:14-16 (PP)
John 3:16 (PP)
John 3:36 (JS)
John 5:39 (SL)
John 6:38 (FS;MS)
John 6:66-69 (TD)
John 10:11 (SL)
John 10:14 (SL)
*John 10:14-15 (SL)
John 10:16 (SL)
John 12:26 (MS)

John 12:28 (FS)
John 13:13-16 (MS)
John 13:34 (CS)
John 14:2-3 (BB)
John 14:6 (TD)
John 14:8-9 (FS)
John 15:1-2 (VB)
*John 15:4-5 (VB)
John 15:5,7 (VB)
John 15:15 (SL)
John 15:16 (RC;VB)
John 15:17 (MS)
John 15:19 (SL)
John 16:27 (FS)
John 17:18, 20 (FS)
John 18:36 (KK)
John 21:22 (CS)
Acts 1:3 (KK)
Acts 11:26 (TD)
Romans 1:18 (JS)
Romans 3:23 (JS)
Romans 6:11(MS)
Romans 8:6 (MS)
Romans 8:28 (FS)
Romans 8:34 (PP)
Romans 9:16 (RC)
Romans 9:23 (RC)
Romans 9:29 (RC)
Romans 11:22 (JS)
Romans 12:17-21(RC)
1 Corinthians 3:10-13 (CS)
1 Corinthians 4:5 (JS)
*2 Corinthians 6:16 (CS)
Ephesians 1:4 (RC)
Ephesians 2:19-20 (CS)
Ephesians 2:21-22 (CS)
Ephesians 5:3 (BB)
Ephesians 5:5 (KK)
Ephesians 5:22-24 (HW)
Ephesians 5:25,28 (HW)
Ephesians 5:28-29 (HW)
Ephesians 5:32-33 (HW)
*Philippians 2:5-7 (MS)
Philippians 2:5-8 (MS)
Philippians 2:9-11(MS)
Colossians 1:13 (KK)
*Colossians 1:13-14 (RC)

*Colossians 3:13-14 (HW)
1 Thessalonians 1:7-8 (KK)
1 Thessalonians 2:12 (KK)
1 Thessalonians 5:17 (SL)
2 Thessalonians 1:8-10 (JS)
1 Timothy 2:1-2 (KK)
1 Timothy 2:5 (PP)
1 Timothy 6:14-16 (KK)
2 Timothy 2:2 (TD)
2 Timothy 2:22 (BB)
2 Timothy 4:18 (KK)
Hebrews 5:8-9 (PP)
Hebrews 10:25 (KK)
Hebrews 11:25 (RC)
Hebrews 12:6-7 (VB)
James 2:8 (KK)
1 Peter 1:18-19 (RC)
1 Peter 2:4 (CS)
1 Peter 2:5 (CS)
1 Peter 2:5 (PP)
1 Peter 2:9 (KK)
*1 Peter 2:9-10 (PP)
1 Peter 2:20 (RC)
1 Peter 3:1 (HW)
1 Peter 5:2-4 (SL)
2 Peter 2:19 (MS)
1 John 1:5 (JS)
*1 John 3:1 (FS)
1 John 3:5 (JS)
Revelation 1:6 (KK)
Revelation 2:4 (BB)
Revelation 14:17-18:4 (JS)
*Revelation 17:14 (KK)
*Revelation 19:7-8 (BB)
Revelation 19:16 (KK)

Appendix 5: Author Introduction

Paul has a great concern over the neglect of discipleship among God's people. He first learned about such a need when working as an overseas church planter during the 1980s. While pastoring in America during the 1990s he developed his first discipleship training material. Later, the Lord called him to establish *Biblical Foundations for Freedom* in 2000. Since then he has been actively writing, holding international Christian leadership training seminars and serving in the local church.

Paul has been married for more than thirty-five wonderful years. With eight children and three grandchildren, Paul and his wife Linda continually see God's blessings unfold in their lives.

Paul's wide range of materials on Christian life, discipleship, godly living, leadership training, marriage, parenting, anxiety, Old and New Testament and other spiritual life topics provide special insights that are blended into his many books and training materials.

For more on Paul and the BFF ministry, check online at : www.foundationsforfreedom.net .

www.ingramcontent.com/pod-product-compliance
Lightning Source LLC
Chambersburg PA
CBHW050133280326
41933CB00010B/1354